River Ride

A solo cycling adventure
along the Mighty Mississippi

DAVID FREEZE

Copyright ©2023 by David Freeze

All rights reserved. No part of this publication may be reproduced or transmitted in any form or by any means, electronic or mechanical, including photocopying recording, or by any information storage and retrieval system, without the written permission of the publisher.

Published by:
Walnut Creek Farm Publishing
China Grove, N.C. 28023

Designed and front cover photo by Andy Mooney.

ISBN 979-8-218-33724-7

foreword

When David Freeze told me a decade ago that he intended to pedal his bike 4,100 miles across the country that summer, I had my doubts.

I've never doubted him since.

David not only covered all those miles in 2013, he also found the energy each evening to type up a report to share with readers of his hometown paper, the Salisbury Post.

The next summer, he did it again, taking a different route. And again the following summer. And so on. At the end of each ride, he gathered his daily reports and other recollections into a book.

This is the ninth book chronicling David's adventures, and it does not disappoint. In addition to following his route beside the mighty Mississippi, this book covers the history of several locales along the way. It introduces you to the people David met on the journey — more good Samaritans and helpful travelers than you might expect. And it details his sometimes comical quest each day for maximum calories and minimal hotel rates. Woe to the motel clerk who tries to charge David Freeze too much.

Burning 7,000-plus calories a day, David naturally develops quite an appetite for food and drink during his travels. (If you ever need to get on his good side, offer him a pineapple milkshake.) His most insatiable urge, though, may be his thirst for adventure. After covering the country coast to coast, border to border, visiting every state and part of Canada, he's probably thinking right this minute about where to go next.

More power to him. Thanks to David Freeze's tenacity — and his talent for storytelling — many of us have traveled vicariously to places we might never have gone otherwise.

Thank you, David, for doing the hard part.

*— **Elizabeth Cook***
Former editor of the Salisbury Post newspaper in Salisbury, N.C.

acknowledgments

I have never done a book that covered cycling trips spread over 15 months before, so I will do my best to include all the many people who supported any significant part in one of my grandest adventures yet.

We rush around every year here on the farm getting things in place for me to be gone for weeks at a time. Those involved in the farm work ahead of and in between both major parts of this adventure and the small add-on to New Orleans included Sam Freeze, Adalie Harrison, Monroe "Booper" Bishop, Clayton Lewis and Aaron Jones. Somehow we always get it all done, and the farm looks passable and remains productive throughout. Others who chipped in were Amanda and Chad Lewis, plus some of Lisa Burleson's big family just up the road, while Ken Bradley was ready to provide security if needed.

Amber Bishop, my youngest daughter, kept the books going. Rayna Gardner made sure that financially we were good, while keeping her special eye on risk management. What if one day she says I can't go because "this one is just too dangerous?" I hope she doesn't.

The long list of sponsors over the two summers included Tim and Linda Hoffner at Father and Son Produce, Dick and Jean Richards, Leonard Wood, David Post, Robin Satterwhite, Luann Fesperman, Frank and Janis Ramsey, St. Paul's Lutheran Church Men's Group, First Baptist Church Men on Missions of China Grove, the South Rowan Y Service Club and Cindy Atkins.

I am extremely blessed to have the Salisbury Post continue to publish these journeys across America. Some changes continue to occur there, but my good friends Paris Goodnight and Andy Mooney carried the load as they found ways to get all my daily reports and many of my photos included in the print version and even more in the online version.

When we began to write the book, my favorite editor of all time, Elizabeth Cook, worked her special magic once again to help me make the words come out right. Elizabeth was the editor at the Salisbury Post when she encouraged and mentored my initial writing efforts. She's the best writer that Salisbury has, and she's made me a better one, along with making each book what it should be, an expression of my wonder in and love of America as I see it by the backroads and even a few interstate highways.

Andy Mooney has a big satchel of special gifts. He's listed as a copy editor, but he has a magical way of laying out a newspaper and a book. He's been with me through all the books and did the cover photo on this one. I always count on Andy for his quiet expertise, and he's made each book just exactly what I wanted it to be.

Where would I be without the readers? As sure as there is a spring, one of my favorite times of year is when the folks begin to say, "Where are you going this summer?" You can bet I've been thinking about it too! Support from the readers, new and returning, guarantee there's a whole lot of my new friends riding along. I've never felt alone on any of this. Thank you, readers, for that!

And finally, once again I will simply say that not one single day of these bike rides has ever started without my special request, "Lord, ride with me today!" To Him, I yield all of each and every adventure.

introduction

Just ahead is one of my bike adventures, a sort of gift to myself. My second favorite mantra is "I haven't been everywhere, but its on my list." You might wonder what Number One is, but I will tell you later in the book.

As we complete the telling of my cycling journey along the Mississippi River and a good chunk of the North Shore of Lake Superior, I almost always write the introduction last. Some readers may also wonder why. I don't want you to miss anything, so we've worked hard to revisit the experience.

Here is just a short recap of what got us here. I crossed the Mississippi several times on other bike adventures. I knew days ahead that the Great River was coming up, eventually just a few miles ahead. Then when I reached it, I was always OK to linger. The Mississippi is special to me, so much so that I have read book after book about it. After traveling most of the more famous cycling routes across our great nation, I thought it was time to reward myself and find out more about that river, from as close as I could get.

I set about planning the adventure, using some material from cycling organizations and more from the books I was reading. July 2022 seemed the perfect time for a journey that could leave out the extreme heat, the exceptionally hard climbing and more of the wilderness rides that readers have been accustomed to over the years. My gift to myself would be just a fun ride, with no strict timetable or route, as long as I could see more of the Mississippi. The river gives me energy for some reason.

You'll see that seldom do I linger at other times, but when the mighty river comes close to the road, I will stop and enjoy what God has made. Yes, you'll read about lots of history, more fine people involved than I ever expected and some lesser heat and climbing.

Have fun riding along, because I had fun already, in more ways than I deserved. I'm addicted to exploring, something that fits my mantra above. My bike today isn't the original, and most of the gear has been changed out for something better over the years, but the goal is still the same. I want to see as much of this Earth as I can, and the most enjoyable way is on a bike seat that I love. You see, that original bike seat has been along on every ride except to Hawaii when I stupidly rented another bike. My seat, a Brooks B-17, has been rained on, nearly frozen, suffered with heat, cared for less than it should have been. Yet it is still as comfortable to me as a car seat or rocking chair might be to you.

Some will remember that my original Surly Long Haul Trucker bike was totaled in Florida in 2014. The seat was one of the only things that survived. It is always ready to go, and so am I. So please join me, turn the pages ahead and let's go ride together while we learn more about America. As always, I am glad you decided to come along!

PART I

chapter 1

How we got here!

Travel has always excited me. A business trip or vacation, especially if I would be traveling to a new area, had the potential to be a lot of fun. As a child, I didn't get to travel much because the family had a dairy farm and always had to be at home morning and evening to milk those cows. There were no days off.

I made a few trips in high school, one to Fort Bragg to stay for a week in hopes that I could attend the United States Military Academy at West Point. We did a few trips otherwise; a memorable one was to the Latin Convention in Raleigh, N.C., while I was a junior in high school. There were a few fishing trips to the North and South Carolina coasts with a favorite aunt and uncle.

Things didn't work out for West Point, but I did get to do some traveling in college with the university band. All this was fun, but I never knew much about the rest of our country. My work life offered a few longer trips, mostly to conferences and conventions. Once I spent January through March in Green Bay, Wisconsin, for a new job and enjoyed it tremendously.

In my mid-20s, I began running seriously. The doors started to open as I became competitive enough to see Canada several times and multiple U.S. cities. Running once paid for a trip to Montreal to compete in a marathon. During the long haul, I spent time in many major American cities and even made a marathon trip to London.

Still, all these trips were somewhat scripted. Get to the destination in time to run a serious race and maybe a day or two of sightseeing before returning home. I loved them all but the focus was on the race, not as much on the new area and there was little freedom to explore.

A few vacations were extensive, such as a driving trip to Chicago to do a race and then lots of historical sites on the way home. Several others were trips that included a marathon while the trip extended into a vacation.

Over 800 running races and many years of playing competitive softball were fun in my 20s through the 40s and into my 50s. Nothing but fun and good memories, but I began to develop a sort of wanderlust and a need to try something exciting. Always an avid reader, I read a long story in the Charlotte Observer about a group of friends who cycled a new rail trail along the Greenbrier River in West Virginia.

I kept that article in my important papers for a couple of years, then decided to head that way on a February weekend with a challenging forecast. I had a Trek mountain bike, a few backpacks and a willingness to try this thing once. The long drive north was in a steady rain, and I considered turning back toward home. But of course, I could not. The drive continued through some beautiful farm country.

The story I've told a hundred times included getting the bike out of my truck and tying two backpacks on the bike while putting one on my back. Ready to leave and ride north for my first ever trip of anything close to 50 miles a day, I jumped on the bike and immediately fell off the other side. Nothing could have been a more humbling experience!

I got back on and rode north through the wilderness country, loving every minute of it. I spent the night in the only real town, Marlinton, on the trail. Rain, off and on, didn't bother me much. The second day, to Cass and back to Marlinton, was a better day, while still cold. The third day had some snow and was the coldest of all. I arrived back at the parking area and at my truck, happy but almost totally exhausted. The scenery had been beautiful, wildlife plentiful and I saw only 12 total people over the three days other than in Marlinton.

I have two lasting memories of that final day of the three-day trip. The first and simplest was that I was starving. I had eaten all the food saved in my bags and vowed to stop at the first convenience store and get a brownie that I craved. I'm sure I got more, but the brownie stood out.

Much bigger as I drove home the nearly four hours that night was how much fun I had. I was truly exhausted, but I knew before I was very far from the parking lot that I wanted to do more of this. Much more in fact, longer than three days and more challenging. Over the next few months, I began to explore the possibility of riding a bicycle across the country.

By now, if you've been following my cycling adventures since 2013, you know I have ridden across the country twice, and I've cycled in every state. All of it has been solo cycling, and I expect to continue to ride alone. Still, I have ridden with other riders for a few hours and even most of a day a few times. Nothing in my life has been a bigger adventure, or now a series of adventures.

I will briefly recap each ride and the part it has played in my exploring so much of America. That first long ride, of 4,164 miles, was from Astoria, Oregon, to Myrtle Beach, South Carolina, over 54 days during the summer of 2013. The route was for the most part the Trans America Trail, famous since 1976 as the most popular cycling route across the country. Spring, summer and fall along this route has a steady flow of cyclists and merchants who expect them. Crossing the Rockies was my biggest challenge, but in every state, other challenges arose. Rain, wind, dramatic climbs, some heat and the most severe storms I had ever experienced up until that time. I was told by an experienced long-distance cyclist not to quit in the first week, no matter what. I will admit some uncertainty and remember some doubt as I looked out the window of the plane when I was about to depart west to start the adventure.

Each early day bolstered my confidence, and finally as

I began the second week, I knew that I could do the ride. One habit that I began on the very first day of this first trip remains. When my bike was put back together, the bike shop operator suggested I take it for a spin and to make sure I rode up the only real hill in town. I did that, but struggled mightily up the one hill, and I was yet to load my 40 pounds of gear on the bike.

The most important memory of that first adventure was that I took the bike back to the motel room and loaded the gear. Then I sat down in the dark room and prayed, "Lord, ride with me today!" Immediately, I felt better about what would happen ahead. That same phrase now ends my prayers every morning while I'm out seeing the country. You'll see just ahead a few instances of why I am sure that God is riding with me every day. I did have serious blood clot issues at the completion of the first ride. These were based on elevation, dehydration and physical stress.

My second ride was done the following year, from Maine to Key West, the easternmost part of the country to the southernmost part of the country. I was never far from the Atlantic Ocean and rode the challenging hills of the Northeast and took on several major cities. I rode through New York City, made much easier because a cyclist that I encountered along the way led me through what he considered the safest route. I had a harrowing adventure trying to find a place to stay on my one night in New Jersey, again led by an angel I encountered. Riding through Washington,

D.C., was a challenge until I hit the Potomac River and less-traveled roads. On down to Virginia and North Carolina, the route leveled out and I enjoyed many days of visits to beautiful beach areas. Terrible roads in South Carolina on super-hot days were tough and traffic was an issue occasionally.

In Florida, in a small town on U.S. 1 called Tequesta, I was hit by a car. While riding through the little town and in a bike lane, I was hit broadside and the car pushed me into the traffic lane. God was with me once again as the van driver behind me was able to see the impact about to happen and she stopped before running over me. Not only did she stop but so did the van in the next lane. The fire department later reported that the last such occurrence between cyclist and car caused the death of the cyclist.

My injuries were minor, although the bike was totaled. Remarkably, both of my shoes were knocked off and one of my socks was missing a quarter size spot in the impact. The fire department took me back to the nearest bike shop about eight miles north where I was able to buy another bike to finish the trip. The bike shop also shipped the damaged bike home. I still have it as a reminder of how blessed I am to still be riding.

By the time I reached Key West three days later, my feet and ankles were swollen again. The wreck and impact to my feet had caused more blood clots which were addressed after I flew home to complete the 2014 adventure.

RIVER RIDE

2015 was the year for my most historic trip, this time from Mobile, Alabama, to Toronto, Canada. Most of it was a re-creation of one of the most popular underground railroad routes for slaves seeking their freedom before, during and after the Civil War. Much of the ride was along the very scenic Ohio River. Once I arrived in Canada, I was actually a speaker at the oldest celebration of freedom for slaves at the Emancipation Day event in Owen Sound, Ontario.

My daughter had dropped me off in Alabama and then joined me at the journey's end in Toronto for a scenic side trip to Niagara Falls and the flight home. No health issue at the end of the ride was a pleasant difference. My bike finally made it home a month later, after being left in a locked FedEx facility for an extended time.

2016 belonged to possibly my most fun ride, along Route 66 from Santa Monica, California, to Chicago and on to Indiana. Traveling through all the small towns of Route 66 fame made a very interesting ride. I passed through the Grapes of Wrath area and eventually fell in love with the movie after riding in the extreme heat of the desert. I also stopped in Williams, Arizona, to visit the Grand Canyon, the single most astounding piece of Mother Nature's work that I have seen. The route through Chicago included a segment of beautiful riding along Lake Michigan. I found Chicago much easier to navigate than New York City, but honestly have found the biggest cities to be easier than some of the lesser ones like Phoenix. Few bike lanes on busy streets leave little room for cars and bikes to co-exist.

Next came another ride that started in the northwest but this time covered what is called the Northwest Tier in cycling circles. Anacortes, Washington, across to North Dakota gave plenty of options for mountains and hearing how the locals favored Bigfoot and any kind of marketing that they could associate with it. Riding during the summer didn't keep me from seeing lots of snow piled beside the road in certain mountainous areas.

I was especially happy with a southerly turn toward South Dakota, where I saw Mt. Rushmore, Deadwood and the Crazy Horse Memorial on the way to Nebraska and Iowa, both beautiful and out of the way enough that I needed to add them on this ride. After Iowa, I ended the trip in Green Bay where I had worked for a long and cold winter. A thousand-mile drive home in less than 24 hours ended that trip, but this time with my bike safely home too. Shipping the bike is almost never easy and seldom works out as well as it should.

In 2018, I got off the bike long enough to run across North Carolina while pushing a baby jogger. From the Tennessee line to the Outer Banks, mostly on U.S. 64, gave me a perspective of the Tar Heel State that few will ever get. I ran on ice and snow in Highlands, saw snow again in Lexington and finished on a warm and sunny Easter Sunday afternoon at Nags Head beach to close out a 42-mile day. Multiple stops by law enforcement concerned that I had a baby out in the cold highlighted the trip. Clearly my "Murphy to Manteo" sign on the front of the baby jogger should have been bigger.

One of the most challenging rides came next in 2019: from Carson City, Nevada, to a segment of California desert, and finally into Canada for the provinces of British Columbia and the Yukon before heading on to Anchorage, Alaska. Long days on the Alaska Highway with few towns, regular sightings of bears and wilderness camping were the challenges of this trip until the day that I was actually chased by a grizzly. Did he want the pie that was in my panniers or did he want a skinny cyclist for a lunchtime snack?

I spent six consecutive nights camping among bear scat and began to appreciate every convenience of an occasional night in a motel room. After being told by other cyclists that I couldn't possibly make Anchorage in time to meet my daughter and son-in-law's cruise ship, I easily did make it. A long ride back to the United States on the Alaska Ferry was another highlight, one in which I slept on deck each night under heat lamps. The largest mosquitoes and flies I have ever encountered constantly dogged me the farther north I cycled.

After Alaska, I had to reach Hawaii for a long bike ride just as COVID was taking off. My only cycling trip of 2020 was a circuitous ride around the Big Island, completed just a few days ahead of Hawaii locking down any tourists still in the state. I saw spectacular sunsets, the lava fields, and the towns of Kona and Hilo while running and cycling parts of the Ironman Triathlon course. A whale-watching adventure, a visit to the volcanoes and riding a rental bike with a seat that I didn't like were other highlights. My 50th and final state was now complete.

Still not done, I decided to ride the southern border of the United States in the summer of 2021. Starting again in California, I never saw another long-distance cyclist on this grueling trek across the hot- weather states next to the Mexican border. One long day's experience in 117-degree temperatures nearly did me in, but after recovering I pushed on toward an encounter with Hurricane Ida and some rumble-stripped roads in Alabama. The trip ended at the Atlantic Ocean, just south of St. Augustine Beach on Labor Day.

And finally, we've arrived at the reason for this book. Part 1 includes the 2022 summer cycling adventure from Dubuque, Iowa to almost New Orleans. You'll read about this journey mostly along the Great River Roads that parallel the Mississippi River and my decision to return in 2023 for an extension of the river adventure, then some added fun through Minnesota to Duluth and along Lake Superior.

My mode of transportation remains the Surly Long Haul Trucker bicycle, tough enough to handle bad roads and heavy loads. Most of my gear hasn't changed much over the last few years. We'll recap what gear choices complete the ride at the end of Part II.

RIVER RIDE

But for now, just settle in for another epic solo ride in two parts. I hope you will enjoy riding along!

chapter 2

The journey begins by car.
Why the Mississippi?

This adventure was going to start much differently than any previously. Most of my cycling adventures have started with a plane ride to a certain destination ahead of many days of riding. On one other trip, the Underground Railroad journey, I had driven a rental car to the start in Mobile, Alabama. On the way, I picked up my daughter, Amber, at a racetrack in Alabama where she and her future husband had gone for motorcycle racing. We then completed the driving trip on a very long day to Mobile, where we spent the night. I left by bike the next morning while Amber drove the car back home and turned it in locally.

My Mississippi River adventure was set to begin with a nearly thousand-mile drive over two days. Allison Tuck, a friend who is also an experienced travel agent, had arranged a rental car through the Concord, N.C., airport, just over 20 miles from my farm. I wanted to leave early, excited for the drive and more excited for the ride along my favorite river of all time. Amber dropped me and the bike off at the airport on her way to work in Charlotte. I waited at the rental car pickup until they opened, then checked in and was given a small SUV that seemed perfect, except that it might not be long enough to fit the bike. I took the front wheel off easily and slid the bike into the available area. Sure enough, there was no way to make it fit. I showed the attendant my problem and was allowed to exchange for another SUV. The front wheel back on, I checked the directions to Dubuque, Iowa, and saw that I would be passing back through Salisbury. I had one mind-clearing stop to make.

Over the years of cycling adventures, my biggest equipment problem had been an ongoing struggle with the cycling odometer, meant to measure my miles without any satellite hookup or cellphone coverage. A simple piece of equipment, the cyclometer was calibrated to the size of the bike wheel so that it could count the revolutions per minute and would thus measure distance. I have always preferred the economy model of cyclometer, but my problem may lie therein. The unit is battery operated and I've become quite practiced at swapping batteries and I always get plenty of notification when I'm soon to need to make a change. Making the perfect connection is tricky, and constant attention to it is required. I didn't want to ride seven miles and not have it noted on the cyclometer.

When taking my practice ride, yes, that's right, my one practice ride on my Surly Long Haul Trucker a couple of days before leaving, I couldn't get the cyclometer to work. I changed both batteries and still no success. The current cyclometer had made several trips and maybe it was just worn out. I stopped at Skinny Wheels Bicycle Shop in Salisbury and was fortunate to find head mechanic Scott available to take a look at it. In my mind, if the odometer could be made to work or was replaced, my driving journey could be a lot more fun. Tracking mileage is critical to the success of using maps and even spotty cellphone directions on the long rides. Wrong turns were seldom fun, although sometimes rewarding with unexpected finds of people and places, But I tried to keep on the planned route as much as possible. Scott replaced the sending unit that mounts on the fork, and it worked. He had already checked over the rest of the bike a couple of weeks before, so I began the long drive in earnest.

I left Salisbury and headed north and then west. On a beautiful day for a drive, I was only delayed once. A near-standstill backup in Charleston, West Virginia, took almost an hour. I never found the reason for the delay but was glad to continue the journey towards another adventure. It had been too long since I dismounted the bike the previous year in Florida.

After a little over 400 miles, I decided to spend the night in Chillicothe, Ohio. Gas was priced right and there were some familiar reasonably priced motels. I drove over to the old downtown area and walked around for about an hour. Many of the stores were open after 6 pm on a nice summer afternoon. The first capital of Ohio when it became a state in 1803 was a good place to spend the night. As I would do often, I picked up my evening meal in an old grocery store. Messages from readers were already coming in with tips on what to see along the Mississippi. I always feel as if I am riding for lots of others.

The next morning, I skirted Chicago while being hit hard by a morning thunderstorm on the way to Dubuque. Light traffic and beautiful farm scenery were highlights on the way to a 2 p.m. arrival. The 1,000-mile total drive was over when I arrived at the visitor center in downtown Dubuque. The sightseeing was set to begin in a big way, because Michelle Rahe took special care to load me up with plenty of information on what I could see in the area. The one single highlight, and what helped me choose Dubuque, was the Field of Dreams movie site near Dyarsville.

Armed with plenty to see in the next 3-4 hours, I took Michelle's advice and decided to get a good sense of what Dubuque is about and how the Mississippi River plays into the city's history. I went immediately to the 14-acre National Mississippi River Museum and Aquarium. A giant operating riverboat paddlewheel dominated the parking area as I headed inside. With lots of windows, I could easily see some of the things outside and felt drawn toward them. But first, I made a quick tour of the inside with most memorable stops at a recreated working shop for all things steamboats. I stood in the wheelhouse of an old boat while a viewing screen showed what an actual passenger on the river would see. It changed from day to night and inspired me to find out more about river traffic including barges and commercial craft, yet still focusing on the historic flatboats, steamboats and shanty boats.

Making sure I made a trip around to see all the exhibits inside the building first, I went to the aquarium for views of the wildlife along the river as well as fish and fowl habitats that included stingrays and alligators. I had a nice conversation with a museum volunteer about what to see after I left the museum. But first, knowing that time was tight for a 5 p.m. closing, I went out back along a river canal to see the William M. Black dredge. Used to keep the river channel deep in the right places, the old ship was huge and similar to a historic navy ship. An onboard machine shop, sleeping quarters similar to barracks for the regular sailors and officers' quarters took up a huge amount of space. An open top allowed for a beautiful view of the area and the two huge smokestacks, which were capable of being lowered to allow the two-story ship to pass under bridges. As you will hear often in this book, the mighty Mississippi is constantly changing course, with sandbars being formed and riverbanks being eaten away. The William M. Black and other dredges were charged with keeping the shipping channel open and as deep as needed. Small boats and large ships had plenty to watch for while on the river, including the opportunities to run aground and be hit by floating and underwater debris.

Various other boats and exhibits outside were fascinating, including the living quarters for families that seldom left their boats. Displays of huge engines and machinery were part of the outdoor exhibits.

The museum volunteer suggested that I not miss the country's oldest and steepest incline railway, located in Dubuque and with a great story. Late in the afternoon, I had driven to a hilly section of Dubuque and found the Fenelon Place Elevator Company. I was about to ride down a long steep hill on a beautifully restored cable car. In 1882, wealthy banker and former mayor and Senator J.K. Graves was frustrated that he could never get a nap at lunch, even though he lived near the bank. Dubuque was considered an hour-and-a-half town, meaning that not much happened for 90 minutes around noon. His ride, by horse and buggy, was slow and tedious on a roundabout route to get up the hill on city streets. By the time he grabbed a quick lunch, it was time to head back without his longed-for nap.

Graves acquired the rights to build a tram car railway to the top of the hill and quickly got it done. Immediately, the banker began to get his naps and his neighbors helped make the little railway a success. The car burned when a fire started from the stove on board, and Graves decided to start charging his neighbors $5 per ride after it was rebuilt. Ten of those neighbors banded together to buy and establish the Fenelon Place Elevator Company. It is still in use today with a phenomenal view of the Mississippi River. I talked the history of the ride with the lady who sold tickets. The ride was $2 each way.

Again, I stopped at a grocery, then found my motel for the evening and also found the airport and drop off for rental cars. The motel game began and is something that I will highlight often throughout the book. There were several motels in the area, but since the airport is really small, none were recognizable by name. I love the motel game, always ready to bargain and even ride a few miles extra to get a good price. As I have said often, all I really need is a clean room, a hot shower, good WiFi and a quiet location. A refrigerator and microwave are pluses. Other than that, I'm good. All I'm doing usually is eating, writing and sleeping in that order. I nearly always leave at first light, so I'm gone before most people are moving. This motel was adjacent to a bar owned by the same man. I have spent the night near bars before and often they can get loud. Not so with this one, and I looked out to notice that the bar was closed by 10 p.m. Few people in the rooms made for a quiet night and the $39 price per night was perfect, not just for one night but for two. Located near the Mississippi and near the road west to the Field of Dreams, I decided to slack pack and leave most of gear in the room for the first day of riding. I would return that evening and load up normally for the first day headed south on the Mississippi.

And now, why was I so interested in the Mississippi? Simply put, I had crossed it several times on my previous bike rides across America. I had a certain affinity for the mighty river and hoped to learn much more about it as I pedaled south over the next several weeks. Two things I knew right off was that about 2/3rds of our country drains into either the Mississippi or the other rivers that supply it. The great river is also very important to the economy of our country, and I hoped to see some of it first-hand.

Referred to as the River of Dreams, the Mississippi River is always at work. I discovered on my first day at the Visitor Center that the Great River Road, or series of close-to-the-river byways, follows the Mississippi River through Iowa. You will read later that I had an eye-opening moment in Hannibal, Missouri, when I discovered that the River Road system (not always the same highway) in fact runs from the humble headwaters in Minnesota to New Orleans, Louisiana.

The Mississippi is one of America's natural wonders, touching 10 state borders while connecting people, places and cultures. A wide variety of terrain, animal and plant life presents itself along the flowing waters, some of it in still pristine and isolated areas.

In 1541, the Spanish explorer Hernando De Soto came upon the mighty waterway as he and his soldiers looked for treasures that could be sent back to Spain. De Soto is assumed to be the first European to see the river. One year later, he died of a fever and was buried along its banks.

The river itself is the reason that the historic villages and cities were settled along its route. Most towns have at least one museum and celebrate their heritage with festivals, parades, fairs and art shows. The Mississippi's economic influence is also evident as barges and towboats navigate the waters. Towboats don't tow their cargo but push it. There are plenty of beautiful bridges, locks, dams, and islands along the way. I looked forward to finding my own way through the various passages along the 10 states that I will see ahead. Besides Iowa, where this adventure started, I will see or pedal through Missouri, Illinois, Arkansas, Louisiana, Kentucky, Tennessee and Mississippi in Part I, then will revisit Iowa before entering Minnesota in Part II.

The Mississippi River is the second longest river in America, second only to the Missouri, extending 2,348 miles from the source at Lake Itasca in Minnesota to the Gulf of Mexico. Sources often provide different distances associated with the complete river and I will share what I heard as the trip progressed. Dredging operations from Minneapolis to Cairo, Illinois, maintain a 9-foot-deep channel for navigation. South of Cairo, the depth is maintained at 12 feet. Below Baton Rouge, the channel is narrow but navigable to the big oceangoing ships. Approximately 15,000 miles of the Mississippi and its tributaries are navigable, used primarily by barges and diesel towboats.

More than a few disasters have been experienced on the river, especially since it is prone to flooding. An ongoing attempt to contain those floods by using a series of levees that are usually at least 15 feet high has been mostly successful.

Floods in 1927 and 1993 resulted in thousands of square miles of land being covered by water. Significant losses of life and property result when the mighty river can't be controlled.

I was ready to go see and learn more about my favorite river.

chapter 3
Field of Dreams and the rest of Iowa

One of my goals since very early in my exploration of America by bike has been to visit the "Field of Dreams" movie site near Dyarsville, Iowa. I rode through Iowa briefly on the way from Washington to Wisconsin on the Northern Tier adventure but couldn't take the time due to a plan for meeting friends and a rental car reservation at the end. Just a little over a hundred miles away that day on the bike, I thought about taking the rental car by there on the way home from Wisconsin. With already a thousand miles to drive in 24 hours, I just couldn't have taken the time to make any real visit. I have watched the movie several times, loving it more each time. Baseball has been a part of my life since a small boy and will continue for the rest of my time on earth. In my opinion, "The Field of Dreams" is the best baseball movie of all time.

After two days of driving and sightseeing, I was ready to ride the bike and get back into my favorite hobby of experiencing America at 10 mph. On my first step out the door, I was surprised by a small rain shower and a lightning strike so close that the snap of thunder was almost immediate. I thought, "Why not? This is going to be bike riding at its best and weather has often been a big element of the adventure!"

First, I needed to drop off the car at the airport and had called to find that the rental car desk opens at 8, so I drove there with the bike still in the car. Most of my gear remained back in the motel room, so I stopped in the provided space and unloaded the bike. Not a single person, but plenty of cars were in the area. Upon my arrival at the desk, I found a sign that said to just drop off the keys in a box provided and a number to call for any problems. I did just that and returned the bike on a partly cloudy morning with a later forecast for heavier rain, very excited to get going.

This area of Iowa is known for its rolling hills, none especially long and not usually terribly steep. However, it is often one hill after another. I knew that from driving in and realized that this was not the part of the Midwest that has those long flat fields. I found the Heritage Trail, an old railroad bed now way more flat than the surrounding terrain and covered with crushed limestone. My legs were not ready for the hills of Iowa, but I knew worse ones would come later when I would pedal into the Ozarks in a few days.

A solid downpour finally hit me as it approached from the west, and there was no cover to be found. First day, first rain and at least that occurrence was out of the way. I met a caretaker of the trail who offered to let me sit in the cab of his truck, but after talking with him for a few minutes from my bike seat, I pedaled on into the rain. It was 37 miles from the motel to the Field of Dreams and I only had to follow the signs at this point. I was ready to see it, rain or not.

Back on pavement, I made the last few turns toward the field as the other traffic was headed in the same direction. I saw the complex ahead, a little in awe of everything that seemed to be happening. A huge number of trucks of all sizes were parked near the major league site as I rode down a very wet road to the information booth. I had been told that entrance to the famous movie site was free, but a woman stopped me to say that I could make a donation of either $20 or $40, or nothing. I told her that didn't know yet and would see her on the way out. I was told to park my bike somewhere near the gift shop and the famous movie house. I did that and walked toward the field with my iPad, ready to take photos of the perfect ball field and that beautiful farmhouse from the 1989 movie. I found out that tours of the house had to be scheduled ahead of time, and since I was soaking wet, I didn't need to mess up their floors anyway. I was most interested in the field where lots of informational signs were posted. I sat on the bleachers, the same homemade ones where Kevin Costner and his movie daughter watched the old players practice.

The field itself is professionally kept up and looks as good as a major league field to this day. The outfield is surrounded by beautiful corn, just perfect for me to walk out of the cornstalks the same as the old players did in the movie. I found a woman standing alone in left field, I suspect taking it all in, who was willing to take my picture. The stalks were wet too, but I hardly noticed.

Once admitted to the area, anyone can go on the field to throw, hit or run. A dozen or so were on the field doing these things when a man walked up to me and said, "Want me to film you running the bases?" I did and he did, making one of most memorable highlights of the trip. Still wet and in soaked shoes, I ran those bases, and no one seemed to care. But I did!

I visited the gift shop and saw some nice shirts and ball caps but decided to leave them on the rack and hangers. I had my lasting gift with a memory for a lifetime.

For explanatory purposes, the Major League field is on the other side of the corn from the movie field, at least 500 feet away. It seats 8,000 fans and on this day was abuzz with activity since the 2022 game would be played just five days later. All those trucks and more arriving by the hour had to do with preparations for that game. I found out just a few days later when watching from a motel that Frank Thomas, former Chicago White Sox All-Star, and some investors had bought the complex from the original owner. They have big plans for college and even high school games to be played regularly on the major league field. The 2021 Field of Dreams game between the White Sox and the Yankees was the most-watched major league game ever at that point.

One interesting sidenote, Michelle Rahe from the Welcome Center is part of the family that maintains the corn around the field. Since I visited in the middle of the summer, the cornstalks were just as they are in the movie. But after harvest in the fall, the field will lie fallow until spring when the corn is planted again.

I pedaled back to the motel, pleasantly tired from the hills and the rain after covering 64 miles. That was enough to make me eat a huge evening meal. I had planned to visit Dyarsville, but the threatening weather had sent me pedaling back toward Dubuque. Dyarsville has a couple of baseball museums that I will see on another day.

It was now time to settle into the late-day routine of eating, planning for the next day, writing my daily update, answering messages and getting as much sleep as possible after all that. I closed out the day writing about a great quote that I saw at the Field of Dreams. "People who know baseball aren't better than everyone else, but everyone else would be better if they knew baseball."

The next morning, I turned my thoughts to the river again and trying to follow a good map of the Great River Road. My motel was on U.S. 61 that would be the primary road as I headed south. A group of connecting roads made up the Great River Road, but more times than not, they didn't follow the edge of the river. Often, they were the closest roads, sometimes because of flooding concerns and other times because there was no road close by. Of course, there are two sides of the Mississippi. Dubuque is on the western side, where I planned to do most of my riding. The earliest maps had more things to see and the closest access to the river. I planned to cross to the eastern side occasionally.

I had realized that morning that I had lost my retainer, the last remnant of the Invisalign process to straighten a front tooth. I was sure it must be in the car and wondered if the car might still be sitting in the same spot at the airport. I rode back to the airport, on my way south anyway, and did find the car still unlocked. After checking between the seats and under them, I could find nothing. I would be without that retainer for the rest of Part I's ride, a concerning problem. Surely the tooth would begin to lose it's way again.

No planes seemed to be moving as I rode the hilly exit and joined back up with U.S. 61. My first turn was onto D55, a lesser road that continued through quaint and beautiful La Motte. Clearly a farming community, the agricultural equipment business was booming but nothing else seemed to be moving. The next intersection was a turn onto U.S. 52 and a National Scenic Highway, part of the Great River Road. At this point, I thought that the GRR was only in Iowa, especially since one woman had told me that I should be very careful while on it. She cited many curves and hills. I got both, expected since I had only seen hilly roads so far in Iowa.

Bellevue was the first real town, with a long main drag

that ran right beside the river, much of it beside an elevated park that seemed a buffer to flooding. These were the best views of the Mississippi to this point, and I took time to stop and eat a large lunch of convenience store food near a memorial to the Union Civil War soldiers who had departed on riverboats from this site. I saw Dam #12, doing its part to regulate the flow of the mighty river. Lots of old storefronts and an unhurried pace on a straight road made me hope for much more of the same as the journey continued.

Next was Clinton, a bigger town with its own baseball stadium, riverboat and even bigger park along the river. Famous for the sawmill industry and logs sent down the river for delivery to them, Clinton had lots going on. A game was being played in the stadium, the riverboat seemed to be loading, and resurfacing was underway on the road to all of this. Very dusty in the area, I rode the park from one end to the other, then retraced my route back to the motel. Bellevue has 2,500 residents and Clinton has 10 times that many.

The ride that day was 71 miles, but I realized the roads that follow the river were not the most direct and added miles because the river is continuously curving and switching back on itself. Right away, I was back in major calorie intake mode with a meal of watermelon, red potatoes, pasta, oatmeal cookies, plenty of water, and likely that wouldn't be enough. I call the process "eating anything not tied down."

29

I was settling into the ride now. Physically I felt fine, and the bike was doing well. Unknown days were ahead, just the way I wanted the adventure to be. Small things highlighting the day included a visit with some dairy cows who followed me and what I considered an amazing performance by a crop-dusting plane. The yellow plane was dipping low over the highway as he sprayed fields of soybeans. I stopped more than once to take photos, not realizing how often I would see the same aerobatics on the rest of the journey. Some 90-degree days were ahead and I knew humidity was a factor too. But still, I was bolstered by the fact that nothing would be as bad as the super-hot conditions of the 2021 southern border ride. A big plus for this area was constant sources of water and food. Towns just ahead included Bettendorf, Davenport and Muscatine.

I went to bed in Clinton thinking I would have a challenging day ahead, traveling thorough one of the biggest metropolitan areas that I would see. Almost 400,000 people make up the cities that I just mentioned. After looking at them on the map, I made up a route that followed the river on less busy streets. I have often heard we spend too much time worrying about the unknown. The more of these trips I take, the less worry plays a part. Still, this one had plenty of concerns since I would be riding in the last part of morning rush hour.

The ride south from Clinton went well on U.S. 67, until traffic began to build. Right away, I made a wrong turn that seemed right at the time when I headed into a huge industrial area. Only about a mile into it, the road dead ended into the parking lot of a factory. I retraced the route and corrected myself until I was directed to a bike path right along the river. Over the years, I have been on lots of bike paths and usually don't prefer them. This one had few other pedestrians, plenty of space and smooth pavement, plus I could see the heavily traveled main road just a couple hundred feet away. There were no cross streets or driveways. A driver had stopped beside me at a light and pointed to the bike path and in a polite way said, "You might really enjoy riding along that bike path," much different than other drivers who often don't want bikes on their streets full of traffic.

Davenport seemed to have done lots of things right. The bike path, river views, elevated walkways across busy streets and well-kept green areas made it one of the prettiest cities that I visited. I had to stop and do a Zoom call for business and did so at a large outdoor amphitheater.

After leaving the metropolitan area, I started looking for State Road 22, and thought I may be on the wrong road. After asking for some help, I found myself a little impatient and just needed to pedal on a little farther. I began to see the heavy industrial side of the river. A series of businesses passed by as I headed toward Buffalo. Heavy rock quarrying, cement manufacturing and grain storage kept the road full of trucks. Near the quarry, the road was so dusty that a water truck was spraying the road. The bike actually picked up a little mud. My view of the river was blocked in this area, but I had begun to see lots of barges that were secured along the river. Empty ones and full ones were both staged for future need and eventual transport.

Pushing on, I rode through Buffalo, Montpelier and Fairport, all small and adjacent to the river. I headed into Muscatine, a much bigger town of 25,000 residents. Soon began one of the oddest occurrences of my trip.

I rode through the small city with beautiful river views. I didn't want to stop in town to spend the night and had more miles in me, particularly since the terrain had calmed down some. When I have cell coverage, I often check for motels or food sources ahead. This was the case in Muscatine when I saw a Super 8 Motel listed ahead, one of two motels according to Siri. I called, got a great rate and promised to be there by 5 p.m. I should have paid attention that nothing else showed on my screen around the motel.

I stopped at a convenience store to get a few snacks and more water, anticipating that this Super 8 might not have a store nearby. I asked the clerk how much farther the motel was, and she didn't have any knowledge of it. Still, I was following the directions and getting closer, so I said, "It should be just 2-3 miles ahead according to my phone." She replied, "I don't think there is anything down that way but some farms and a big hill." Now I was concerned but knew that something had to happen with phone directions soon.

RIVER RIDE

Back on the bike on a nice afternoon, I heard Siri say, "stay in the left lane and turn left ahead." I could see across the median and just ahead was a left turn. I turned left with one nice ranch house in sight and soon she said, "Arrived!"

Nothing was ahead for miles, at least too many to ride ahead. I called the other motel a couple of times, and nobody answered. Still, it was my best option. I rode back toward Muscatine and followed directions to the nearest motel with no one answering still. Tracking the directions back to town took me a different way, where I soon found the motel. Like many of the small locally owned motels, this one had changed over to a residential status, meaning that renters kept their rooms for a long period of time. It looked completely full and was. A note on the door explained the situation. I would have to find another motel in town. Two other motels had closed, and options were limited.

I found a Travelodge, one of those that wasn't the cleanest, most friendly, or anything else because it didn't have to be. It had been a very long day of 85 miles, about 20 of it used for an out and back 10-mile ride which I would have to do again the next morning. It's all part of the adventure of solo touring on a bicycle. I wouldn't change a thing, leaving it all to experience and a better outcome should the same thing happen again. I have often received puzzling directions from Siri, and then usually change over to Goggle's office assistant when that happens.

Next up would be more riding on U.S. 61 to Burlington,

Fort Madison and Keokuk, all still in Iowa and on the river. My night in the Travelodge passed without incident and I headed out for an even longer ride on Day 6 of the journey along the Mississippi. Forecasts of 95 degrees seemed of little concern as I again remembered the 117 degrees experienced on the Southern Border ride. Back on U.S. 61, I pedaled back past the same convenience store and Siri's ghost motel site for the third time in 12 hours.

U.S. 61 would likely be my route for most of the day. I passed Wopello and another closed motel before the road added rumble strips, both on the side and in the middle. The whole road isn't very wide and the cars crossing the middle rumble strips to avoid me are going into the opposite lane. This makes for a tense situation sometimes and all a cyclist can do is trust what is happening behind them. I'm so sure of that, as I have mentioned before, I won't wear a rear-view mirror.

Next town up was Mediapolis, surrounded by agriculture but with two odd things. Very small, it had a large and very new convenience store on the right and an old, very busy one on the left, just across from each other. One of the few other businesses in town was a Family Dollar and Dollar Tree combined in the same storefront.

On the way to Burlington, the rumble strips went away, and cycling became easier. Burlington was one of the first state capitals of Iowa and is a city of about 25,000 people. With a booming downtown and plenty of traffic, my route of 61 South continued right through the middle of town.

Just before entering Burlington, I saw a person waiting on me at the top of a busy heavy-traffic hill. I pulled over since he was standing by the road in front of his truck and smiling. Rick Luckenbill is a long- distance cyclist too, and he offered some advice. One was that I could exit busy 61 South where he was standing and take a couple of less-traveled side roads and eventually end up intersecting 61 again. He also suggested I would enjoy riding a detour along the Mississippi River towards the back way entrance to Keokuk. His words that I remembered the most were, "There are a couple of hills along the way, but it is a very scenic road." Troublesome words to be remembered later that same day.

I didn't see Fort Madison, the next town, because 61 South bypassed it with plenty of exits available. Soon, I had to decide whether to follow Rick's advice and detour through Montrose. Sometimes open to a little more adventure than I should be, I took a left and followed the scenic drive. The two hills that Rick mentioned were hard to define because there were about five gut-busters. I did cross a small bridge right away that had concrete planters on both sides filled with flowers, a first for me. Montrose was very small, and I asked directions to make sure of the right exit from town to follow the river.

The first short and steep hill came just on the edge of town as I passed houses on an incline with beautiful views of the river. The hills kept coming as I pedaled toward Keokuk, the southernmost town in Iowa where the Des Moines River empties into the Mississippi.

With about 10,000 residents, Keokuk sits on a knoll above the river. The climb uphill was the most challenging of the ride yet, causing me to wonder which of the hills made Rick's list. Certainly, with plenty to choose from, I finally spotted the Chief Motel and my room for the night. I had talked with Alpa there several times and was assured that she would hold my room even though I was arriving after 6 p.m. The Chief Motel was the best of the motels so far and offered plenty of variety after a super challenging 91-mile ride. Just across the street was Dairy Queen and my favorite pineapple milk shake. Across the opposite street was a well-stocked modern grocery, so I was quickly set for the evening. I was just ahead of leaving Iowa the next morning and excited to keep the trip moving.

Looking back at Keokuk, first started in 1828 as a trading post, I found out that the Clemens family once lived in Keokuk after they left Hannibal. Samuel, who became Mark Twain later, helped publish the first city directory in 1857. Other famous people with connections to Keokuk included Teddy Roosevelt, Andrew Carnegie, Betsy Ross, Robert E. Lee, William Jennings Bryan, Carrie Nation, Roger Maris, the Marx Brothers, Buffalo Bill Cody, Howard Hughes and John Phillips Sousa. The town is named for Sac Indian Chief Keokuk.

chapter 4

Missouri and Mark Twain

With a hot forecast still a concern, I pedaled south from Keokuk for some of the best and flattest riding so far. A simple two-lane road with little traffic was perfect for the morning. Too early to leave the hills behind for long, I found them again as U.S. 61 bypassed Canton, just after crossing into Missouri. I was getting quite hot and thirsty as the highway tried to bypass Palmyra too, but a big truck stop was right at the top of one of the longest hills.

I was far from the only one headed for the very busy truck stop, although few were likely to get a caffeine-filled Diet Mountain Dew and energy-boosting Reese's Cups for the push on into Hannibal. Most evenings and mornings, I help to pass the time on the bike seat while envisioning how the next towns ahead would look. From the first planning for this ride, I had read about Hannibal and couldn't wait to see it.

With all the talk about the Mississippi River, Mark Twain, Huck Finn and Tom Sawyer, I thought sure that my idea of a big town right beside the water had to be right. My first sighting of modern Hannibal was about two miles from the river and very busy with traffic and chain stores. Knowing I had to get out of the hills and head to the river, I hoped that much of the ride would be downhill, and the last mile was. A steep decline into the old town brought me to a world reminiscent of Twain's time here.

Motels were abundant, but some of the economical ones were a little too far out to see the river. In my mind, I envisioned the Country Hearth Inn would be a nice place with a river view. But realistically, I suspected it wouldn't be because the price was too good. I coasted right past the visitor center and on to the motel. The sign was broken and not many people were there, making me wonder if I had better look for another motel choice. I stopped and checked the possibilities on my phone and decided to give the Country Hearth a shot. Inside the office, I met the owner, who was excited about my bike ride and even discounted my price from the posted rate. I would spend a full day here touring the town, only the second time in 50 states of solo travels over 12 years had that seemed proper. I already knew of a handful of things I wanted to see, and on this Sunday afternoon, I went back uphill to the visitor center shaped like a riverboat. Inside, I got the travel guide with information for the area and began to put a plan in place.

Not sure that I was satisfied with the motel, I asked at the visitor center if there were any unusual places for a long-distance cyclist to stay. The attendant mentioned a homeowner on the steepest hill in town who had a several apartments

RIVER RIDE

that he offered for a great price. I already had seen the steep hill, but I was still intrigued. She called the owner, couldn't get him and then gave me the number to keep trying. I did call him and left a message but never did hear back.

The Country Hearth Inn turned out to be OK other than the WiFi, which kept going in and out. I told the owner, and he came to the room and said it was fine. It was, when he was there. For the rest of my two-night stay, I relied more on a sparse signal from both AT&T and Verizon, both which could be made better if I held made better if I held the phone or iPad up to the picture window. My photos and my newspaper updates made it out barely.

I had an interesting discussion with the motel owner too about animal danger stories. I told him that my ride to Alaska had involved being chased by a grizzly. Sam, the owner, had barely escaped death when being charged by two elephants while cycling with a friend.

Food came from one of two well-stocked convenience stores, both just a few blocks away. I couldn't see the river from my room, but I was just one right turn away from it and the most historical part of Hannibal. Nearly everything was labeled Mark Twain this or Samuel Clemens that. Fine with me since I am a big Mark Twain fan. My plan was to do the old Hannibal trolley tour, ride the Mark Twain Riverboat and visit Mark Twain's Cave. Plus, whatever I discovered while spending a full day here. Maybe a stop at Twain's boyhood home if time allowed. Only twice have I spent two nights in the same town while actively on a bike ride, in Hannibal and Williams, Arizona, gateway to the Grand Canyon. I hoped Hannibal would prove as interesting as Williams had been.

After a good night's sleep, I decided to walk to Mark Twain's cave, home of both the sightseeing and cave tours. I thought I had worked out a plan on how to see all I wanted to in a day, according to the town's tourist site map. The cave appeared to be just past the city limits, which I had seen the previous day. Hannibal wasn't big and walking seemed much better than taking the bike and worrying about it still being where I left it. As a lot of tourist maps do, I found that some creative license had been taken since the walk turned out to total about three miles round trip, even after getting best directions from a resident. The morning was hot and humid, making for a sweaty walk especially when I realized I would miss the first sightseeing tour, crucial to staying on schedule for the day.

After finally arriving at the cave site, I checked in at the desk and realized that by blind luck I had ended up with the cave tour first. Immediately after the cave tour, I could step right onto the next sightseeing tour. The desk attendant sold me both for a package senior discount, even better than I expected.

Both tours were first class, beginning with the "always 56 degrees" cave. On a muggy summer morning, I was glad to have the jacket while in the cave. The cave was found when

RIVER RIDE

a dog fell into a hole and his owner went in after him. It was used as a hideout by the Frank and Jesse James outlaw group, but I wondered how they could be comfortable in such a chilly place. Twain supposedly spent lots of time in the cave and included it in some of his writings. The cave tour took about an hour.

Just as expected, I was able to step right on the tour vehicle and head for Hannibal next. Only another tourist couple and I were on the bus with the driver and the tour guide. I totally enjoyed the tour, also about an hour in length, and got my bearings on how I would spend the rest of the day. We didn't step off the tour vehicle, similar to a WWII army truck, but we kept going up and down all the historic streets. We rode through the old downtown and heard how Twain's family had early beginnings there, then on to see the Twain lighthouse from a distance and the famous Huck Finn/ Tom Sawyer statue just beneath it. We heard about how all the big riverboats used to stop in Hannibal, and a revival of the same thing was currently occurring again due to the expansion of the dock area. Most interesting to me is the growing interest in riverboat travel along the Mississippi, so much that the Viking Cruise Lines out of Europe would soon have a boat plying the busy river. For the first time, I saw examples of how the Mississippi River is constantly shifting and changing its flow.

With a good grasp of what I wanted to see, I walked back to the dock area and paid for my riverboat tour. The boat was small and perfectly scaled for a scenic cruise on the river. The afternoon breezes felt great as we cruised up the river, then back down and finally returned to the dock. Along the way, I saw Lover's Leap, a 200-foot overlook where a young Native-American couple supposedly leapt to their deaths in a final desperate attempt to be together. We saw massive barges with a towboat pushing them up the river. Barges are so much more economical than trucking, especially for locally produced products like grain and concrete. We could easily see the Mark Twain Memorial Lighthouse atop Cardiff Hill. I later walked the 244 stair steps to the lighthouse base.

Also very interesting was that Mark Twain was first employed as a riverboat captain. But when other riverboat captains were told that they would be conscripted into service to haul Union soldiers to and from battle, Twain decided to change his employment to a writer and would eventually head west to the sites of some of my previous travels in Virginia City, Nevada, and San Francisco, California.

Late afternoon was approaching, and I had two more goals. I went to the famous "free ice cream cone a day" hardware and got one. In the back of the store is a large self-serve soft ice cream dispenser complete with sleeves of small cones. Nobody monitors the ice cream dispenser, but the store was jammed full, selling all kinds of touristy things. Marketing at its best.

My other goal was to visit the Tom Sawyer fence where

the fictional Tom enticed his friends to whitewash because it was such fun to do. I noticed a couple taking photos of their brush strokes and asked them if they would use my iPad to get some good shots of me. I was genuinely excited to whitewash Tom's fence. The couple was from Arkansas, and his name was David too. They asked about my bike ride and wanted to know where I had been previously, exploring more possibilities for sites to see during their vacation week. David and his wife were especially interested in the God moments that happen on my rides. Those 15 minutes spent talking to them were the best of my day!

Next, I got a photo of Mark Twain's home but didn't take the tour. Twain was born Samuel Langhorne Clemens in 1835, two weeks premature, and was often a sickly baby. The Clemens family moved to Hannibal from Florida in 1839, where they opened a store that went bankrupt. The family built their own house in 1844, the same house known today as the Mark Twain Boyhood Home. Financial problems forced them to move out in 1846. Sam's dad died suddenly in March 1847, but his mother was able to collect some debts and moved the family back into their home. Sam was forced to leave school at age 12 and found employment with the local newspapers. The family left Hannibal in 1853, Sam to St. Louis and the rest to Muscatine, Iowa. The family never again resided in Hannibal.

The next biggest sighting on this day was a sign that showed that Hannibal was on the Great River Road in

Missouri. At this point, I didn't know that the Great River Road extended to other states besides Iowa. So excited to see if a Great River Road map existed for the rest of my cycling trip, I called the visitors' center to ask. The attendant said, "Yes, and I think I have a copy or two of it here." I told her to hold one for me and walked back up the long hill past my room and returned to the visitors' center, especially grateful to find a copy of the exciting map set aside for me. I now, from that moment forward, could follow a route planned by someone much more knowledgeable than me as I headed to New Orleans and the end of this particular journey. Another surprise was the fact that the Great River Road was depicted on both sides of the river. I planned to cross the river several times and hit more states whenever I could find bicycle-friendly bridges. Swapping back and forth to follow the river more closely will extend this current trip by a day or so.

On the way back to the motel, I stopped to walk around the "Unsinkable Molly Brown" house, a museum open several times a week but not at the time when I was standing in front of it. Molly is remembered for being on the Titanic, where her bravery helped save other passengers as she implored the sailor steering her lifeboat to pick up as many survivors from the freezing water as possible. Many of the lifeboats did not pick up those in the water for fear of running out of room and capsizing. Many lives were lost because there were not more Molly Browns.

RIVER RIDE

From the beginning of planning this journey, I had expected to avoid as much as possible of the several major cities on the route. But I had a change of heart with the Great River Road map and a better explanation of how to get through St. Louis in a couple of days. While watching the coverage of the Field of Dreams Minor League game, a day ahead of the major league game, I thought back to how wonderful it was to run the bases there and to have it recorded on video. As of this writing, I have not yet rewatched the movie itself but can't wait to do so.

Three choices of how to leave Hannibal and head south were rolling around in my mind as I went to sleep last night. I could cross into Illinois near Hannibal or retrace my tracks back to U.S. 61, or I could take U.S. 79 directly south from old Hannibal and see more of the river. All three would be hilly because Missouri is proud of that adjective, but I wouldn't have to backtrack to leave town on U.S. 79. I chose U.S. 79.

On the way out of town, I retraced my route past the Mark Twain Cave with a couple long and challenging hills. The morning was cool and foggy, but still humid. I again passed Lover's Leap and the half-mile-long hills continued. The highway was in the process of repaving, something definitely needed. I passed several scenic outlooks which would have required more stout climbs. I had completed only 35 miles by noon when I rode into Louisiana, Missouri, a perfect spot to stop and eat a convenience store lunch along the river.

Back on U.S. 79, I pedaled through Clarksville, Annada (with a population of just 29, all unseen) and on into Ellsberry. I had called ahead to the only motel nearby, especially important because it set up my next day's ride through St. Louis. Yes, I had decided to take on a big city, ready for the excitement of battling traffic. The day's ride totaled 59 miles, not enough but the best choice possible on this day.

What made the stay in Ellsberry most memorable was the motel. I had called ahead several times and finally got to speak to someone who said she was in charge. She wasn't sure she would have a room because most of the motel was a habitat for those staying a longer period, not usually a good sign. I fortunately checked into a room, and immediately realized that it needed a significant cleaning even though the room itself had been remodeled in a pleasant way. The woman in charge was so scattered and the general appearance of the motel was so poor that my ride to find food also included a stop to add cleaning supplies to my needs. This has happened more than once on my adventures, and those times will always be remembered. Good thing the ride was not significantly challenging or my arrival later in the day. I value the time off the bike almost as much as the pedaling during the day, but some cleaning had to be done.

Ellsberry has 2,000 residents and the Dollar General was one of the best I have seen, complete with produce and plenty of good snacks and microwaveable food for the evening. Ice cream is always available in DG stores, and I was ready for some.

The room had dead bugs in some places I had expected and a few more. The floor had not been swept in a while, so I began there. I found the sheets clean, and the room didn't smell smoky, both big pluses. I cleaned the room, sprayed a pleasant air freshener and left the remaining supplies as a donation to the motel, wondering if anyone would use them. I got enough WiFi to submit my story and photos for the day before getting food and supplies, so it was finally time to relax with my food while planning for the next day's ride. I watched a little TV, answered some emails, and went to bed early while thinking about my upcoming entrance to St. Louis.

My goal as I loaded the bike the next morning was to get an early start and follow a route that would enter the city through lots of suburbs on U.S. 79, then eventually join my old friend U.S. 61 later in the afternoon. I didn't expect any sightings of the river today. I had a city map that was detailed and felt good about the challenge ahead.

Ellsberry was very quiet as I left town on another cool morning. Still in Missouri, the Ozark-like hills kept coming, and much of the riding time there included no road shoulder. Riding in traffic became quite spooky as the morning rush into the city continued.

Foley was the next community. I knew something important must have been there because we had to stop at a stop sign with no side road. So very unusual that I didn't know exactly when I did pass through Foley. Winfield came next with a couple of convenience stores. The best thing about the next town, Monroe, was a much better road. Traffic was quite heavy as we neared the greater St. Louis area.

I stopped at a McDonald's in the first suburb called St. Peters, and talked to Jerry, an off-duty employee. He asked about my bicycle and route, saying that he would love to do the same thing. Especially since he blamed fast food for making him overweight and had decided to make a big change. I made my first turn onto city streets with plenty of traffic on what was Missouri 364, a state road serving as an expressway and connector across several of the neighboring suburbs. There was so much fast-moving traffic that the roar was quite loud, often made this way when lots of vehicles are moving fast on concrete. The shoulder was wide and good as I raced along, usually stopping to dismount when crossing the fast-moving exits and entrances. I waited my turn to run across while pushing the bike, then remounted for the ride ahead to the next one.

Prominent on the map was a route that continued south by using U.S. 67 on the way to merging with U.S. 61. Daily I was realizing that U.S. 61 would come and go but remained prominent in the Great River Road odyssey along the river. St. Louis is tremendously hilly and has lots of stoplights, meaning that I stood waiting for the light to change before trying to use the low gears to climb the next hill. Briefly we rejoined the Lewis and Clark route. Other than Missouri 364, which used long grades for faster speeds, U.S. 67/61 kept a progressive roller coaster going,

    I began to think of a place to overnight, ready to get most of St. Louis behind me and enjoy the evening. One perfectly situated and reasonably priced motel was already full, another that used online registration was just too costly. A Quality Inn in Arnold was on the route south, and for fun I called and actually got a person to answer at the desk. I told Tina what I was doing on the bike, and she gave me a wonderful rate and said they welcome cyclists. Tina gave me a route, but in an effort to shorten the route, I involved Siri. This was a mistake since she got a little confused and had me ride across the interstate and then told me to turn around and take the interstate. After riding a couple miles out of the way, I was ready to take a chance and called Tina one more time to find out if bicycles could ride the interstate in Missouri. I remembered about six years ago on another summer adventure that I couldn't get a straight answer to the same question in Missouri. I called the nearest bike shop and couldn't get a straight answer either, so I rode my longest ride ever, 120 miles, on Missouri interstate without a problem.

    Tina did answer again and said she didn't know about bicycles on the interstate, but if it was her, she would pedal as fast as possible since their exit was just over four miles away.

    I jumped on the interstate ramp and pedaled onto I-55,

only needing to ride a fast 4.5 miles and avoid any policemen. I came flying down a long hill and spotted a police car parked at the bottom of the hill with the driver's side door open, all lights flashing. I have been stopped more times than I can count by state troopers, deputy sheriffs and policemen, and it looked as if this might be the next time. But as I neared the police car, I realized another car and its driver were just ahead and slightly off the pavement. That driver appeared to have a sobriety problem and the officer never looked over at me as I continued on by, pumping my legs as fast I could go.

The ride ended at a fantastic motel, Tina's reasonably new Quality Inn, situated in the middle of every type of food that I might need. Tina was wonderful, just as she sounded on the phone. And the room was fantastic, no cleaning needed on my part. I grabbed the perfect meal at Waffle House and some small things at Walgreens. Then came a wonderful evening of reporting, planning and eating, all done as a mish-mash together. The day's ride totaled 71 miles and I felt exhilarated by the whole day. A couple of days' riding was left in Missouri and the major league Field of Dreams game was the next evening. I had to find a great place to watch it.

For the first time, I-55 and U.S. 61 were both designated the Great River Road. I-55 would be faster but wouldn't get close to the river, so the next morning I asked directions from two local painters and found the best way back to U.S. 61. I found it to be another road with endless rollers and often no shoulder. The drivers waited behind me while I climbed, or they went around me if space permitted. No horns of frustration. Then as the road got busier, U.S. 61 added rumble strips forcing me into the traffic lane at all times. The close exposure to traffic was horrendous that morning.

I passed through Bernhardt, Pevely and Festus. Only Festus had much, and it had everything. I didn't miss a chance to load my bags with food. I'm continually hungry on these rides, especially if the traffic issue is a challenge. I'm on edge so much that I seem to burn extra calories. After passing through Bloomsdale, I noticed that the map seemed to show that I would see the river in St. Genevieve and St. Mary's. I called the local welcome center and found that I would have to backtrack and take another road north to see a sort of harbor, but that I might be disappointed. The she said, "And you might as well forget about seeing the river in St. Mary's too. The river used to run right past the town, but the river had since shifted east." She told me to ride out on a side road on the Kaskaskia Bridge and look at the dry riverbed where the Mississippi used to be. St. Mary's was a town that used to be too, and very little remained after the river's departure. I was about to turn farther from the river and end a very poor day of river searching.

With another 14 miles or so to reach Perryville, I had long uphills that were wearing me out while I pedaled very tight roads with endless traffic. I saw a sign for I-55 and decided to join the interstate for the last part of the day's ride. The final six miles were a breeze compared to the challenging and less scenic 68 miles that I rode that day. Nobody seemed to care that I was riding a bike, so by that time I was pretty sure that the state didn't either. Missouri must still be interstate bicycle friendly, but I never had a flat stretch the whole day.

I found my motel and settled in for another pleasant evening. Perryville again had nearly everything I could think of that might be needed. I enjoyed watching the Field of Dreams game, but it wasn't nearly as interesting since my New York Yankees weren't playing this year. I was clearly focused on seeing Cape Girardeau, the next definitive tourist spot ahead. I would definitely see the river. Hannibal, Camp Girardeau, Vicksburg, Natchez, Baton Rouge and New Orleans were the towns and cities where I expected to gather history and spend a little extra time. I had planned this during the late spring and early summer and got on mailing lists and email alerts for what to expect.

Cape Girardeau was the home of Rush Limbaugh and a Roswell-type alien crash, and the city is loaded with other history. I read that it had a magnificent waterfront and I wanted to explore it. I would explore the city and decide afterwards how to proceed.

Two things broke on this day, a lock down strap on one of my pannier bike bags and the foot cage on one of my pedals. I couldn't repair the bag but had options of how to tie it shut. I wasn't too worried about the foot cage but knew that I needed it to help provide leverage as that foot pulls the pedals through the pedaling cycle. Both feet push down on their own, but the cage provides the ability to lift the pedal on the opposite side of where the pedal is pushing down. Without a real plan, I just kept riding. I would get a new set of pedals at some point.

Good weather was forecast ahead and there had been no real rain since the opening day of the ride in Dubuque. I left the motel and immediately jumped on I-55 for a faster and less hilly ride of about 35 miles to Cape Girardeau. I rode hard with the trucks on another cool morning and found myself standing on the waterfront before noon. I had stopped at a very busy convenience store where cycling enthusiast Dale Nittinger filled me in on all things worth seeing locally.

Those things worth seeing and knowing about in Cape Girardeau included an early visit by Lewis and Clark, action from the Civil War and more Mark Twain history. That history spread over nearly 300 years. In the 1730s, a young Frenchman named Jean Baptiste Girardot established a trading post on land jutting out into the river. The site was called the Cape. By the mid-1700s, Girardot had moved on. In 1793, the Spanish government gave Frenchman Louis Lorimier a sizable land grant which included this region. Lorimier is considered the city's founder, yet the name came from Cape and a derivation of Girardot's name.

A highlight of the Lewis and Clark expedition was a visit to the Red House in 1803 for dinner. The Red House is still standing, yet it was built when the thriving settlement included about 1,111 residents. Steamboats and railroads contributed to the small village's growth into a city.

All of the waterfront has a flood wall completed in 1964 with huge steel doors, ready to be closed to seal out the rising river. Murals are painted on the inside of most of the flood wall, and a specific area just on the other side of the wall is best for just watching the river flow. I saw river business underway, with towboats pushing the barges up the river.

On the south side of town was the magnificent and modern Bill Emerson Bridge. I rode across the bridge into Illinois, surprised to see how flat the land was as far as I could see. I wondered if most of Illinois was like that, so different from the endless hills of Missouri. I checked the map again, but none of the roads on the that side of the river were closer and none kept me going better toward the other scenic towns I had planned for. I called and booked a Super Eight Motel in Sikeston, Missouri, another town familiar from my years working in horticulture and grass seed procurement. Missouri is huge for production of Kentucky 31 Fescue. I just turned around and pedaled back across my favorite river.

I made it to Sikeston and was surprised to see that another Super Eight Motel was much older, although still very nice. The rate was good, but the room was small enough that it was a struggle to get the bike in the room. I went from a 5-pillow bed to only a 3-pillow bed this time, and I am sure that those things matter to someone. I've never figured out how to use a bunch of pillows while alone. I rode a mostly good 71 miles today.

Readers often send me tips on places to see. Sikeston has the Lambert Cafeteria, something that I saw advertised on a billboard, also in the room and heard about from a couple of friends. It is a sit-down cafeteria where they don't leave a breadbasket on the table but toss you a roll when you ask. They have been doing this for years and have quite a following. Just half a mile away, I passed it up for a quick pick-up of a Burger King Impossible Whopper Veggie Burger, fries and ice cream across the parking lot. I thought it would be quick, but found the doors locked. Only the drive thru was open, and I had to walk through the car line and get my order. A first, but worth the effort. Not much else caught my attention in Sikeston, but the desk manager told me not to miss New Madrid, with lots of history and a beautiful waterfront. I was about to see one of the most interesting towns and hear the most miraculous story of the whole trip.

I went to sleep thinking of my last day in Missouri, and how enjoyable this trip had been so far. I was excited to see what the day might bring in New Madrid. To save time, I rode a segment of I-55 to the best exit for New Madrid. A total ride of 22 miles that early morning got me to the waterfront with a walking path along a levee that would serve for flood control when needed. The Mississippi was especially beautiful that early morning, and a wooden overlook got me even closer. Immediately I saw historic signs and a cannon that referred to the Civil War battle where 20,000 Union troops assaulted New Madrid and her two Confederate forts in March and April 1862. One of the forts was on Island #10, which has since been washed away by the everchanging river. With their victory, the Union forces controlled that part of the river for the rest of the war.

Most surprising to me was the statement that "Old Abe," a live eagle mascot of the 8th Wisconsin Infantry, was actually on hand during the battle. I saw a bigger-than-life statue of "Old Abe" on an earlier bike ride through Wisconsin and found that the eagle had been present in major battles at Vicksburg and Corinth, Mississippi. "Old Abe" was carried on a special perch throughout the Civil War and lived through 37 battles and skirmishes.

I took an hour for a tour of the New Madrid Historical Museum. Administrator Jeff Grunwald was the perfect host, and my bike was a conversation piece as others came and went. In addition to local history and the Civil War happenings, I learned about one of the most interesting stories I've ever heard on my cycling adventures. In 1811, one of the world's most powerful earthquakes ever was centered near the town. New Madrid sits on a fault line that spawned the major earthquake and more for the following year. Since the initial quake, another 5-25 are felt in the area each year. In the initial quake, reports were that the Mississippi River briefly flowed backward. Some scientists support the claim, saying that the upheaval actually did change the course of flow for a day or two. Reports of feeling the same quake came in from as far away as New York City.

Today, New Madrid is a happy and beautiful little town of about 3,000 residents, several of whom stopped to talk when they saw my loaded bike. Museum administrator Jeff told me that the hilly riding was over, that I would experience nothing but flat all the way to New Orleans. Jeff also told me that cyclists had always had a hard time getting into and through Memphis, but he thought something had been worked out. We'll discuss later how both of those predictions turned out.

By late morning, I was back on the road. I joined U.S. 61 and then went back to I-55 before passing through Portageville, calling itself the soybean capital of the world. Somehow, after seeing a bunch of these claims over the years, I wonder if another town didn't also claim the same thing. Perfect weather and a tailwind pushed me on for about 50 more miles toward Blytheville, the first town in Arkansas and just about five miles across the state line.

As I entered Arkansas, I was not sure if I could ride on the interstate yet again. Just five miles to go meant another "push it hard and repent if needed" ride but again no one seemed to care. The interstate quality lessened and more trash began to show up. A theme was developing: the farther south, the more trash. I stopped at a wonderful welcome center for more information before pedaling on. The attendant told me, "I've never heard that you can't ride your bike on the interstate here."

My amazing trip continued, and I was still full of anticipation.

chapter 5
Arkansas, Tennessee and Mississippi

I had previously called ahead to the Super Eight Motel in Blytheville, expecting to go three in a row at this usually affordable chain. I left my name but did not make a reservation, which turned out to be one of those very lucky decisions. I pedaled up to the front door of the motel and immediately thought twice. No one was at the front desk; the front door was locked and it looked like all interactions had to be handled through a small window with a buzzer on it. Lots of unsavory characters around, several broken down cars and plenty of trash were easy to see. What wasn't easy to see, of course, was what the rooms looked like inside. Suspecting that I had better find another place, I called around and thought I had talked to the desk person into a deal at the America's Best Value Inn. Less than a half mile away, I headed that way.

I found the motel, noted that it looked nice and that it appeared to be undergoing a renovation. Inside, I met Dana, one of those down-to-earth people who genuinely wants to help. No one else was around, the parking lot didn't have many cars, but the office looked spectacular and appeared recently redone. I told Dana that I had just called and had seen an interstate sign offering a special. Dana told me that she couldn't offer the special rate, but she could do another one and I would be in one of the most recently renovated rooms. I took the deal, got directions on places close by for food and thanked her. Lastly, she reminded me there would be a real breakfast the next morning in the lobby.

As I usually do, I unloaded some of my pannier items in one bag and the other full bag and left them in the room before heading out to get some things to eat. Dana had told me about a Waffle House close by, always a favorite and good for quick replacement carbs. I found one named the Waffle Inn, but it was closed that evening for some reason. I settled for what was becoming a staple, the Impossible Whopper, fries and ice cream from Burger King. Then I rode to a convenience store for more bottled water and some snacks for the evening and for early tomorrow. I met Jaimee Williams at the checkout. Since no one else was around, she asked about my ride and showed genuine interest in doing something similar. With my bag loaded to the brim, I headed back to the room to get my writing underway, totally happy with my situation that night after 79 miles of pedaling. Jeff from the New Madrid Museum, Dana and Jaimee were three of those people that I love to meet across America. Just another great day in America on a bicycle!

Back on the bike early the next morning, I pedaled around to the office to get my breakfast before leaving. I leaned the bike against the wall and walked inside. I didn't see a breakfast and the desk clerk was a guy who was just sitting on a sofa until I walked in. I asked about a breakfast, and he seemed suspicious and wanted to know what room I had come from. I couldn't remember my room number and had to look it up. The clerk said, "OK, tell me what kind of eggs do you want, I can make them." Thrown off balance by the whole thing, I just laid my key card on the front desk and told him that I would find something on the road. I told him how nice Dana had been the night before and his attitude certainly was lacking something. Looking back, I guess there were not a lot of people at the motel and waiting to prepare the breakfast was a cost-saving thing. The farther I rode the less I was bothered by the 'no breakfast' morning.

My first four miles were on I-55, then I joined U.S. 61 at a junction of the two roads. U.S. 61 in this area had a great shoulder, almost no traffic and beautiful farm scenery. The TV weather that morning called for significant southerly winds, meaning that I was probably in for my first headwind of the journey. Prevailing winds across our great nation are more often from the west and when riding south, a westerly wind serves as a sidewind. Today was expected to be the exception. I truly was in flat farmland now and all the flatness adds to the wind's intensity, just another part of the adventure.

U.S. 61 in this area was signed regularly with reference

to Americana Music Highway. BB King and many others from the Memphis area had helped shape Blues music over the years. Traffic was light as I pedaled through a long series of very small towns, including Bardette, Luxura, Osceola, Driver, Wilson, Bassett, Joiner, Frenchman's Bayou, Terrell, Clarkedale, Jericho and Sunset. That run ended when I turned onto State Road 77 at Marion, a productive and busy town.

I kept seeing what looked like high levees to my left, but never saw any real access to the river. I stopped at a convenience store in Osceola and asked a customer if there was a possible sighting of the river in town. I was told there was no opportunity to see the river except from a few industrial sites, and the roads ahead would lead away from the river.

My focus was on making West Memphis and how to cross the river and enter Memphis. I found some articles online about a railroad bridge with pedestrian access added but struggled to figure out the best way to make my route to the bridge. Once I knew the name of the Harahan Bridge, I was surprised to find that Siri knew the way. The high bridge had actually been repurposed for pedestrians in 2016. Jeff from New Madrid was right, cyclists did have a way to cross the river. I also found that cyclists were prohibited from every other bridge entry into Memphis.

I used a mixture of city streets, with a couple of hiccups, and a nice bike path to access the bridge while traffic from I-55 and I-40 buzzed all around and sometimes over me. I pedaled up the bridge access and found a parking area for vehicles complete with picnic tables and restrooms. West Memphis had done this right. I pedaled farther up on the bridge, never a steep climb, and saw that trains were still running just on the other side of a see-through fence, probably less than 30 feet away. I stopped at the top of the climb to take photos of downtown Memphis with the Mississippi River in the foreground, one of my favorites from the trip.

Once I exited the bridge, I found access to the city streets blocked by moving trains. Again in a sort of pedestrian park, I asked one couple, then another before I was told how to get out. Right away, I needed to find U.S. 61 and Siri again came through with good directions. U.S. 61 appeared to be a main thoroughfare, sometimes six lanes wide but with plenty of traffic lights. I was just a few miles from Graceland and the Peabody Hotel, both favorites from a yesteryear running of the Memphis Marathon. With a friend, we stayed at the Peabody where the ducks have a long-standing tradition of coming down the elevator and heading for a fountain. On the marathon course, we had the opportunity to run up steps onto a flatbed trailer for photos with 1960s-era cheerleaders and Graceland, Elvis Presley's home, in the background.

Late in the day already, I wanted to find a decent motel on the way out of town while headed south on U.S. 61. A continuing series of older motels in various states of repair were mostly on my right as I pedaled away. I called several and asked for rates, finding that I would pay as much for one of them as I had for one of the chains recently. One motel desk wouldn't give me a rate until I got there. I spotted one that looked good from the road and stopped to ask the rate. I found two grumpy guys who told me I couldn't lean the bike against a wall. I took the room, but once inside, immediately went back to the office. The room had not been cleaned, was clearly a smoking room and had the oldest TV I had seen in years. I went back to the office and asked for a refund. Both men refused, but I told them I would make a few calls about it and wait here until I got the refund, one way or another. Then one of the guys wanted to show me another room, which I looked at and saw no difference. Finally, I got the refund, likely because they were used to fighting this battle and I seemed persistent. I rode farther south and called another one, surprised to hear an upbeat younger woman answer. The price was better, and I told her that I would be there in a few minutes. Upon arrival, another locked office door made me wary, and I asked to see the room, a request that she declined. I told her that all I needed was a clean and quiet room, nothing special. She held my credit card while I went to see the room and yet I found it suitable.

After paying for the room, I rode to the nearest convenience store, one of what seemed like dozens along that part of U.S. 61. My luck turned when I found fresh pizza, good prices on water and ice cream, and very pleasant staff.

At least I was going to eat well, even including a wonderful price on watermelon chunks.

After 80 miles, I settled into the room, and my writing and food. I got to see the Yankees play baseball and the only drawback was that they lost. Later a smoke alarm started going off about 2 a.m. I pulled the battery and went back to sleep.

The next morning was warm and especially humid. I got back on U.S. 61, happy to be leaving this city. I left at sunrise but still found plenty of traffic riding along, up and down some surprising hills, and in a big hurry. Just as soon as I left town, I found the state line for Mississippi.

Mississippi kicked off with rumble strips forcing me into traffic, never pleasant. Thankfully the traffic lessened and was always forgiving of me taking a lane. Some of the road was in poor shape and in need of maintenance. I passed through North Tunica and what seemed like a golfer and gambler's paradise. Some tall casinos could be seen in the distance to the west. Then came Tunica itself, first notable by a welcome center that included a blues museum. Upon entering, I was told that all the maps and information out front were free and so were the bathrooms, but if I went past them then I would have to pay $10 to tour the museum. I stopped at the bathrooms but did enjoy the blues music that was playing on a quality sound system.

I took time to read the reasons that Mississippi was notable. Mississippi claimed the first PTA, the first female rural postal carrier, the only petrified forest east of the Mississippi (Flora), the most Miss Americas, the invention of Pine-Sol, the Towboat Capital of the World (Greenville, but according to the visitor center, I was later told it doesn't touch the river), the International Checker Hall of Fame, the Cotton Capital of the World (Greenwood) and the Sweet Potato Capital of the World (Vardaman). I found no ex-wives on the list of notable Mississippians, a good thing.

Newly armed with a better Mississippi map than what I had before the welcome center, and the massive list of notable Mississippians in case I ran into any of them, I headed back out to the bike. I noticed that the day was getting hot and would likely be the hottest to date on this trip. Tunica only had about 1,000 residents but seemed much bigger. They had a huge convenience store/ truck stop where for some reason I was craving potato logs and got a few plus a giant iced drink.

Back on the road, I pedaled south on a mostly in need of repair road with little or no road shoulder. An extra trial of a building headwind was pushing me backwards. A long and hot uninterrupted 50 miles of riding was my only goal, already in search of the next convenience store. Most of the scenery was dominated by huge fields of crops that included some mature corn, soybeans, cotton and rice, all in very good shape.

Just short of Clarksdale, I stopped at the first convenience store I saw, almost desperate for ice. This segment of my trip reminded me of America's southern border trip from the previous summer, marked with an unusual craving for ice and almost any kind of cold drink. The first thing I found was an ice machine out of order, then next a locked bathroom, both not helping my plight much.

My luck began to improve as I entered Clarksdale. I had called the Quality Inn around midday and was given a good price by the front desk attendant. Traffic was extremely heavy, but I was able to cross the highway and lean my bike outside before entering the most needed air-conditioning of the trip. I waited for the front desk person, a different one from before and now a large and happy appearing Black man. I told him I had called about a room and been given a certain price. The man introduced himself as Shaquille and immediately set up my reservation. I told him that I had stayed in several Quality Inns recently and he helped me set up a Choice membership to get even better pricing ahead.

Shaquille was genuinely interested in my trip and asked how he could help. I told him that I could use the opportunity to wash some clothes if they had a washer and dryer room. Shaquille said he did but would rather I just give him what I had that was dirty and he would wash them for free along with some other things from the motel. I asked about an ice machine, and he said one of the two in the motel was not working, but he could bring me all I wanted. And he offered to give me a very expensive water bottle that would keep my water cold all day if needed. All this while taking care of other front desk happenings.

Later when he brought my clean clothes by the room, Shaquille asked if he could call ahead and secure a good price on any Choice member motels ahead. I thought I wanted to head toward Greenville, if the town touched the river, but because of that I was not sure of my route over the next couple days. Impressed by Shaquille's effort, I decided that I would look for Quality Inns ahead, especially since I was now a Choice member.

True to my history, I began to crave more ice cream as the temperature warmed. One very timely reader said, "Why are you not eating as much ice cream as you usually do?" Honestly, I can say that the temperatures had only become hotter in the last few days, but possibly the most important reason is that the South Rowan Y Service Club had not offered to fund my massive ice cream input as they had last summer. Once this issue was published in my latest column, the service club reinstated my lifetime ice cream funding but only while on a bicycle adventure. Some details are yet to be worked out, but we do have a verbal agreement.

I pedaled away from the Quality Inn and was very thankful for the wonderful evening of catching up and planning ahead. I started south again on usually friendly U.S. 61, all the while planning to make a call to Greenville to find out what I might find should I ride there. I waited until I thought the visitor center might be open.

Still battling rumble strips, I pedaled south in the driving lane and passed by exits for Duncan, Shelby, Winstonville, Mound Bayou and Merigold before hitting the busy town of Cleveland. Cleveland had everything for its 12,000 residents and bicycle riders battling the building heat. Afterwards came small towns Boyle, Shaw and Leland.

While in Leland, I called ahead to the visitor's center in Greenville. I was very politely told that the town itself did not touch the river, but I could see it from a couple of casinos and a park south of town. I decided to stay on U.S. 61 and get a good jump on my journey to Vicksburg.

U.S. 61 cut down to a two-lane road and no shoulder, just south of Leland. It was a beautiful area of agricultural crops and I especially enjoyed seeing a yellow crop-dusting plane on and off all afternoon. I last saw him 50 miles south of where I saw him warming up earlier that morning. The pilot was like an artist at work as he dipped down low over the fields and then gracefully pointed the plane upward just as he reached the tall trees that bordered the fields.

Winds had not been a factor all day, one of the reasons that the crop-dusters were at work. Late in the day, I noticed two things happening. Lots of hay was being baled and combines were running hard to harvest corn, just ahead of what appeared to be a massive storm system heading my way. The wind changed and for the first time on the trip, gusts made me work really hard to keep going. I saw the corn combines still going hard, too, even when it looked like the storm was just minutes away.

I had a bigger dilemma. I had called the Cotton Country Inn and arranged for a room earlier in the day. The room was way too cheap, but no other options seemed available. I wondered what kind of room I would find. Still on U.S. 61, I asked Siri for directions and hoped she knew them. The bottom was ready to fall out of the storm and the clouds were spread across the whole eastern horizon. The combines were shutting down and huge tarps were used to cover the bins and wagons of corn.

Sure that the motel was close by, I followed Siri as she told me to turn right and that the motel was just a quarter mile ahead. I pedaled up to a building that was definitely not the motel, and thankfully had a couple of people to ask. They told me to get back on the U.S. 61 and keep going for another couple miles and the motel would be on the right.

Blowing drizzle was falling and I pedaled as hard as I could until I spotted an old-style motel on the right, very plain and with only a few cars in its gravel lot. My $40 room was in the motel, somewhere. As I turned into the gravel lot, lightning began to flash all around. I pedaled under cover of an awning and called the number, telling the lady who answered that I had a room but couldn't find the motel office. Very kindly, she told me that the office was in front of a white car, which was hers, and to come on down. Now, with the steady rain falling among more lightning and loud thunder, I ducked into the office. The woman in the office said she didn't have my name, but the price was right. I paid her, got a key to a room and entered an obvious smoking room. Though clean, it smelled of smoke in a big way.

I went back to the office and the woman told me that she didn't have non-smoking rooms. Then she thought a minute and said that one of the long-term residents didn't smoke and I could go check that room out. She walked with me, and we looked in. Small, with no smell of smoke, and obviously better than the now raging downpour, the room seemed OK. I asked about food in the area and the office attendant told me that all the community had was a Dollar General and a small Stop and Shop grocery.

While waiting out the storm, I realized that I had good WiFi and a great supply of ice, and I was lucky to have the room. I didn't ask, but I reasoned that transient farm workers must use this motel because there were very few other businesses except for the huge farms. Starving, I was ready to go find the grocery as soon as the rain lessened to a steady drizzle.

I followed directions and found the grocery store in Hollandale. It seems that much of the town's population was in the very small store and no one was in much of a hurry to leave. I had a couple of nice conversations and grabbed a few things to fill my stomach. Oddly missing was any supply of bottled water. I realized that Hollandale probably was the poorest town that I had ever seen, yet the few things on the shelves were in great demand. Amazed at how everyone in the store was talking to someone else, I grabbed my things and headed back to the motel.

With darkness coming, I prayed to safely make it back, although there was little traffic. I made the turn onto U.S. 61 and nearly threw myself off the bike as the front wheel slipped into a deep open gap between concrete slabs and forced an immediate change of direction. Only a cyclist would notice the gap and be bothered by it at all. I was extremely glad to not have damaged the bike or been injured myself.

I returned to the room, made a little bit of microwave food, had some ice cream and a few snacks and went to bed early with thoughts of going to Vicksburg the next day. Vicksburg was rumored to be one of the most beautiful Mississippi River towns and was immersed in history. I was ready to see it.

Up as early as there was light on a cloudy and humid morning, I slipped out of my room and certainly didn't bother any of the other 3-4 rooms being used. I walked my bike on the wet gravel to the highway and again began pedaling south. There was no shoulder, but with little traffic and a good flashing rear red light, I felt safe any time that I heard a car approaching. As the light improved, I began to see quite a few grain trucks rolling past me. Most of the traffic seemed farm-related, and I passed one grain elevator that had many of those who had passed me waiting to unload. I imagine much of what was on the trucks was the late day corn combined ahead of the big storm yesterday. A listed town called Panther Burn passed by, but I thought it looked more like a huge farm.

Next came a little town called Nitta Yuma. I saw one car moving in the community as I passed by but then realized that all the buildings were very old. I looked up Nitta Yuma that night and found that it once had about 600 residents and most of them did not want any part of the community to modernize. I found that many of the buildings were from the 1700s.

Just ahead, I got a great breakfast deal on a couple of egg, cheese and tomato biscuits at a convenience store. The store was busy because intermittent areas were being paved along U.S. 61 and the workers seemed to be stopping in for breakfast or snacks. Rolling Fork, Cary, Valley Park and Redwood passed by with some good stores for ice. About 40 miles of the day's ride was on freshly paved asphalt, the best kind of riding. None of the new paving was getting rumble strips and still the traffic was seldom heavy.

I stopped to talk with one of the flagmen who held up rows of cars until they could pass while using the lane that was not being paved. My head filled with memories of flagmen who wouldn't let me ride through new paving areas, but no problems materialized. This flagman, Quentin, was extremely interested in my ride and wanted to know how he could follow it. He promised to do so, and I headed on south. Quentin cautioned me to be aware of trucks coming but to just get over if a long line of traffic came my way.

My riding for the last few days had been through the Mississippi River delta, very flat with no hills. In fact, I couldn't remember when I had seen the last one. Hadn't Jeff from the New Madrid Museum said, "Nothing but flat from here to New Orleans!" I took him at his word, but it was not to be. Jeff did tell me that he had hardly ever ridden a bicycle.

As I approached Vicksburg, hills came back. I shouldn't have been surprised because the strategic reason that the city was so important to both sides during the Civil War was that the bluffs of the city provided high ground to allow cannons to control the river. When I reached the outskirts of Vicksburg and the Yazoo River, I saw two major hills ahead after 60 miles of pancake riding for the day. A sign just ahead pointed right toward downtown Vicksburg. My maps suggested that I should keep riding straight ahead, but I wanted to be sure and stopped at the Country Junction Restaurant to ask. I saw owners and mother and daughter, Sue and MacKenna, who were outside mowing the grass and about ready to head back into the restaurant. I asked which way to downtown Vicksburg and they both suggested the hard right just ahead on a road that appeared flat. But they did say, "It is about the same one way or another; you're going to get hills either way."

I took the downtown exit off U.S. 61 and immediately found that most of the traffic took the same exit. The road was bad, pitted from so much heavy truck use on the way to the Port of Vicksburg. After a challenging up and down ride of about six miles, I finally saw the river just about the time that the downtown area began. All the streets ahead seemed harshly uphill.

The river was not the Mississippi but the Yazoo. The Mississippi River used to be here but moved away, and the Army Corps of Engineers diverted the Yazoo River to accommodate light shipping. On the river, I stopped at the Jesse Brent Lower Mississippi River Museum, a huge building that also served as the town's welcome center. I was surprised to find out from the two ladies inside that Vicksburg doesn't have city tours, something that floored me. Why not, with so much history and the National Military Park close by? One of the ladies was in charge of admission to the museum and the other was an employee of the welcome center, but neither seemed surprised that there were no longer any tours.

I toured the huge museum and the Mississippi River IV, a huge towboat and link to the commercial life of the Mississippi River. My tour lasted about an hour, and I thanked both women as I walked the bike up the street. Historic houses were all around me, but I didn't have a good way to find out about them. I decided to head on up the hill towards the Vicksburg National Military Park. By the time, I reached the park and its visitor center, I had just enough time to watch a movie about what happened in the area. A fascinating story, especially since the town's residents ended up suffering right along with the soldiers as the Union forces tried to starve them out.

The importance of Vicksburg in the Civil War was like no other city, except possibly Richmond. Confederates controlled the river with 172 guns and riverfront artillery batteries. Defenders used the swamps and bayous for a natural defense and roads for supplies and troops. Vicksburg was the South's lifeline.

If the North could gain control of Vicksburg to add to their other captured areas north and south of the city, Lincoln knew the war's end would be hastened. He called Vicksburg, "The key. The war can never be brought to a close until the key is in our pocket." The Federals had captured post after post, but Vicksburg had to come next.

The Union Army attacked several times and couldn't take the entrenched town because the Confederates held the high ground. President Lincoln and General Grant decided to "out camp" them, blockading the city so that no food could get in. Eventually the Confederates had to surrender and with that it gave up control of the Mississippi River, virtually splitting the Confederacy in half.

One telling piece of information that I later discovered in the Vicksburg guidebook was the size of the two cemeteries in the area. The Vicksburg National Cemetery, near the northern end of the Military Park, includes the burial sites of 17,000 Union soldiers, a number unmatched in any other national cemetery. The Cedar Hill Cemetery contains the graves of 5,000 Confederate soldiers who died during the Siege of Vicksburg.

Federal troops remained in Vicksburg until President Rutherford B. Hayes removed them at the end of Reconstruction in 1877. Their lingering presence was a bitter reminder to the residents of the South's lost struggle for independence. Some residents resented and challenged the troops while others welcomed them in hope that normalcy would be restored.

Under military rule, Vicksburg's residents faced suspended civil liberties and had to recite loyalty oaths. Property was seized, arrests were made and some citizens were banished from the area. Over 5,000 United States Colored Troops were garrisoned in Vicksburg. Many stayed after the war and the end of Reconstruction, when some opened banks and churches and entered politics. Still, their own freedoms were limited, even after Mississippi was readmitted into the Union in 1870.

To get into the military park, I used my national park lifetime senior pass purchased out west several years ago for $10. Since then, I have used it over and over and have never been refused at any national park location across the country.

After talking to one of the rangers about the locations within the park, I found out that the park would close at 5 p.m. except for walkers, runners and cyclists. I had one special site that I wanted to see in the park, the USS Cairo, one of the first ironclad gunboats. The Cairo sailed up the Yazoo River, then north of Vicksburg, on a mission to destroy Confederate batteries and clear enemy obstructions from the channel. Suddenly two quick explosions tore holes in the boat and in minutes, it sank. Only the tops of the smokestack and flagstaff remained above water. Amazingly no crew were hurt. Cairo was the first vessel ever sunk by an electrically detonated torpedo. Silt, sand and mud covered the ship until its 1956 discovery. Like a time capsule, the Cairo had preserved information on naval construction, naval stores, armament and the crew's personal gear.

The boat's remains and artifacts are on display at the U.S.S. Cairo Museum, near the back of the park. Already at 5 p.m. and knowing that I had about a 10-mile ride to see the outside of the museum and probably the boat itself from a distance, I opted to see this portion of the park on another visit later. As hilly as the park is, I estimated at least 3 hours for the total roundtrip to the museum, a time that would put me exiting the park after dark. I had writing, planning and eating to do that couldn't wait that long.

I decided to head for my motel for the evening, yet another Quality Inn. After taking a left turn back toward the motel, I noticed that a truck stopped on the side of the road just ahead of me. Layne Logue, a civil engineer and wilderness canoe expedition leader, stopped to offer me water and to find out about my ride. After we discussed my cycling, I asked him about expedition canoeing. Layne takes big canoes out on the Mississippi and goes camping on the sandbars. It all sounds like great fun to me, something hopefully that I get to do one day. Later that evening, Layne sent me some great suggestions for the rest of my trip including what to see, and where to stay and eat.

The Quality Inn in Vicksburg was fairly new and was the best room of my trip. Trina, the front desk person, told me not to miss the breakfast. I promised not to. Day 16 of this adventure came to a quiet close with another Waffle House meal and lots of good messages from the readers. Natchez was just ahead.

Overnight, while in the cozy room, I heard a very loud clap of thunder. I didn't think much of it until I heard the forecast. Showers early and heavy rain for much of the day. I looked out in the dark at 5 a.m. and saw that we already had rain falling. Light rain is almost pleasant to ride in, especially when the temperature is warm, and even heavy rain has made for some great adventures over the years. Just the previous summer, I came off the highest mountain of the trip in New Mexico during a huge downpour so bad that the road was flooded such that I couldn't follow where the road was. Nothing like this was expected on the way to Natchez.

I mentioned to Layne Logan, the civil engineer, that I was surprised about how challenging the hills were in this area. He said that a long series of faults were the reasons for the hills and most of the rest of Mississippi would be challenging. Heading south from Vicksburg, I found U.S. 61 to be four lanes and light traffic after I reached about five miles from town. As the rain increased, the visibility decreased, yet everyone seemed to give me plenty of room. Rumble strips all morning pushed me into the lane and only once did I have an issue.

Occasionally I would pass a beautiful old mansion in the distance, although none were close to the road, and I couldn't make good pictures. For a very long stretch there were no businesses and only lots of trees and a few cars to see. It is at these times that my thoughts take over and I'll admit to some daydreaming while the pedals are turning. Suddenly from behind me, I heard a car's tires squealing while sliding. The sound stopped just behind me, but just then I noticed a teenager in a beat-up small car slowly pass me with what appeared to be his phone camera recording. Shaken more than I want to admit, I had plenty of time to think about what had just occurred. I think the driver thought it would be cool to try to scare me, film while he was doing the deed, and then drive slowly by in triumph. I was more shaken right after this happened than when the grizzly bear chased me in the Yukon.

The first town today was Port Gibson, with lots of beautiful homes and streets in need of repair. Civil War history quotes General Grant as saying, "This town is too beautiful to burn!" Even with the steady rain falling, Port Gibson was beautiful and I'm glad that Grant saved the structures.

RIVER RIDE

As I was leaving town and just before stopping at a convenience store for a bathroom break and snacks, I noticed a sign that said, "Natchez Trace Parkway." I had heard a lot about the parkway, known for its beauty, low speed limit and no trucks allowed. The parkway stretches for 444 miles and is sort of a Holy Grail for touring cyclists. When I saw the parkway entrance, I was way tired of riding in the lane due to the rumble strips and tired of getting splashed by the vehicles passing me. The rain had intensified and was near downpour status.

I checked my maps and found that the parkway would not increase my distance to Natchez at all and it was also marketed as having no tough inclines. Layne Logue had suggested I try part of it before reaching Natchez. I decided to give it a shot, even with no stores available the rest of the way. I wouldn't need any water because I was being doused with it every moment of the ride. I told Layne I didn't like cycling trails where a rider is shut off from civilization, but the parkway appeared to be like a very well-kept linear park.

What I found was some of the best riding of this trip. My only real concern was the constant heavy rain was causing creeks to flood to near roadway height. Otherwise, the parkway had some long grades but nothing steep, much better than U.S. 61, which it crossed at least twice that afternoon. With no real concerns for traffic or anything else, I made up some time lost with the earlier steeper climbs. My total mileage on the parkway was 31 miles. I joined U.S. 61

just as it passed through Washington and entered Natchez and joined the rush through town toward the Mississippi River. As it turned out, the rain had lessened and the hills didn't get any worse before I found the Deluxe Inn for a great price, just a mile from the river. I saw two beautiful bridges, one going to Louisiana and one coming from there, over a swollen and muddy Mississippi. I grabbed some food at a nearby grocery and talked to two other guys staying at the motel for work purposes. Then I went inside to do my daily report, plan for entering Louisiana and the last 185 miles of the trip. This was a wonderful 78-mile day, rain and all. Rain was still a possibility for tomorrow and the roads continued to get worse, the farther south I went. U.S. 61 will remain my road of choice for most of the remaining trip. I had begun to think of U.S. 61 as the Great River Road but also in the same vein as Route 66, an old friend.

The terrain around Natchez on the Mississippi side of the river is hilly. The city sits on a high bluff above the Mississippi River and to reach the riverbank, one must travel down a steep road to the landing called Silver Street. Many wealthy plantation owners had land in Louisiana but chose to have homes on the higher ground in Natchez. Prior to the Civil War, Natchez had more millionaires than any other city in the United States. Today, Natchez boasts more antebellum homes than any other city in the U.S. because the Civil War largely spared it.

After the fall of New Orleans and Vicksburg, Natchez

surrendered to the Union Army and General Grant established temporary headquarters in what is now called Rosalie Mansion. Slave trading ceased in the city in 1863 after the Union Army occupied the city. It is commonly thought that as many as one million slaves were traded or passed through Natchez. Hundreds of people living in Natchez during this period, including many former slaves and refugees, died of hunger, disease or were killed in the fighting.

Post-Civil War, Natchez survived on cotton and logging. Today, tourism is important to the city. The old Warren County Courthouse, which was a target for many a Union gunner, still stands on one of the highest hills in the city. The courthouse is where Jefferson Davis learned that he would be president of the Confederacy.

Two firsts for Vicksburg are interesting. Until 1884, shoes were not designated for the left or right foot. A shoe was just a shoe and not form fitting. Past that point, shoes were sold in pairs. Also, even though Coca Cola was invented in Atlanta, it was first bottled in Vicksburg.

My last morning in Mississippi began with a long climb to get back to U.S. 61 and then another challenging six-mile climb to reach the top of what was called the Big Hill. Slightly dark and foreboding because of the clouds, my red light on the back of the bike seemed to keep me safe. I found a booming convenience store with an awesome price on two quickly delivered egg and cheese biscuits while exiting Natchez.

My morning goal was to make the Louisiana line about noon and figure out the rest of the day afterwards. I passed through Woodville, the only town of the morning, and found the state line at exactly 12:03 p.m. It wasn't raining and I had just one state to go, a state that would complete part one of this cycling adventure. I hoped there wouldn't be any more of the dreaded rumble strips but plenty of good roads. I was partially right.

chapter 6

Louisiana and New Orleans

Imagine my mood improvement when I saw the Louisiana state line, complete with new, better pavement and a wide bike lane on the side. One of my favorite photos of Louisiana was the Mississippi Road with no shoulder and rumble strips ending at the state sign and a much better road ahead. I was excited about the ride into New Orleans, just a couple of days ahead if all went well.

The weather was improving along with my mood, and just past the state line was a sign for a welcome center. Speaking to a qualified person when entering a new state almost always helped with my planning, and any new maps were worth checking out. Often welcome centers had the very latest and best maps, plus sometimes inside information on any road issues and occasionally insight into good prices on motel rooms.

I pedaled into the welcome center and not a car was around. I checked the front door and found that the welcome center was closed due to lack of funding. This should have been a sign of things to come. Remember the lack of funding when I recount the cycling past Baton Rouge towards New Orleans.

Small towns just past the state line included Laurel Hill, Wakefield, Bains and Hardwood. Nothing was happening in the towns as I continued to spot antebellum mansions along the highway. Their placement suggests that some form of road had preceded U.S. 61 as a popular byway for 200 years or more. Many of the mansions were now bed-and-breakfast operations.

Aware that my panniers were quite full, I decided to stop at the first post office I saw and send some things home. Another unusual occurrence happened when I saw a post office, not really in a town, and with only one car in sight. It was hot and humid, but I gathered up the things I wanted to mail home, went inside and waited to ask the postmaster what size of prepaid box would work best. The woman looked at me, and admittedly I looked wet and maybe a little dirty, and she kept talking to someone about her personal issues. Not especially happy that she had to put her call on hold, the postmaster said, "How can I help you?" I told her about my ride, and why I needed to ship some things home. She told me, "The boxes are right over there. You pick one and go ahead and pack your box." By the time I asked to borrow tape, she was back on her call. I was the only customer, and I began to laugh to myself about the situation. I took the biggest box, and filled it up without taping the bottom, with hopes that she would soon end the call. She pitched the tape onto the counter, and we finally made some headway. I sent all the brochures and other collected information, my sleeping bag, some unneeded clothes and two tire tubes. Why I did that seemed logical. I had three more tubes still in my pannier. After way too long, and a payment of $21, I left with much more room to better pack for the train ride home.

The afternoon remained hot and sticky, but the forecast called for serious storms to resume soon. Occasional showers fell, but nothing even worth pulling out my rain jacket. As always, a little rain helped to cool me and the asphalt under me.

Finally, I had Baton Rouge ahead. The clouds started to intensify ahead, but well ahead. I suspected the blue and black clouds were already battering the city, and eventually I would tangle with them. I had a good map and tried to figure the best place to spend the night. I made a call, didn't get the rate I wanted and tried again. I couldn't find any small motels on the route and decided to call the Comfort Inn, a Choice motel but nearly always just above my intended price range.

Watching the storm ahead, I decided to take it head-on by trying to find a room and beat the storm to it. I stopped to call the Comfort Inn and ask the desk clerk to give me a rate since I was now a Choice member. Precious, the clerk, told me that she couldn't give that rate over the phone. Becoming more than a little frustrated, I watched the lightning ahead as I held a stopped bike. I told Precious that I was in a bad situation and just wanted to know what the room would cost so I could get a plan in place. She responded with a price that it would be if my Choice membership was approved once I got there. I took the deal and began to pedal south as fast as I could. Traffic was heavy as we had now entered the first part of rush hour. The storm continued to look worse, and I still had about ten miles to ride.

Just about that time, I noticed something on the other side of the four-lane road that deserved my stopping once more for a photo. The journalist in me always comes out when there is a story or an important photo. Underneath a dozen tarps or more were a bunch of people and what appeared to be a huge number of belongings. I saw no vehicles but imagined that those belongings, if that is what they were, had to be on carts. I'll never know any more, but with the heavy rain now just minutes away, those people seemed to be ready to wait it out. There was so much material that it would have easily filled a tractor-trailer.

I had an immediate need to ride fast. Right away, I got caught by a couple of stop lights, and realized that I was heading toward the Baton Rouge airport. Once I cleared the stoplights and made a left turn, I didn't have much traffic. Now it was simply up to me to outrun this impending storm. A beautiful rainbow was off my right shoulder where it appeared the storm had already been and gone. So pumped that I could pedal about 15 miles an hour on flat ground, I was watching my odometer to count down the distance. I spotted the Comfort Inn and wheeled right up to the front door, which had a small overhang, not the kind that cars can drive under. I leaned the bike against a corner of it and ran inside. I immediately spotted Precious at the desk. She said, "I was praying you would make it. Is it raining yet?" Just at that moment the bottom fell out in a driving downpour. I asked if she minded if I brought the bike inside and just got it inside as the back of the bike was getting wet. I had beaten the storm and was even more pumped.

After the bike was inside, Precious told me she had a room but that she couldn't get the lowest price although she was very much in the ballpark. I was just glad to be inside as the rain pounded down outside. Lightning flashed and thunder boomed. I asked about any place to get food because all I could see was the airport. Precious told me about a convenience store a half mile away. I relaxed and ate a few cookies while writing my update.

Later that evening, I walked down to the store on the flooded streets. Every car that passed was spraying water, so I walked in the wet grass. My only source of food was a minimally stocked convenience store. Lots of things were in boxes, but there was little besides cookies, crackers and snacks to choose from. I couldn't decide if the store was closing or just opening. I did get a pint of Blue Bunny banana split ice cream.

Back in the room, Precious called to make sure I was happy with the room. I told her I was and that I was also happy with my day that included 85 miles of riding and all the fun that goes with it. I listened to the Yankees play baseball on my iPad and drifted off to a wonderful sleep as I anticipated one more day of riding to New Orleans.

Baton Rouge's metropolitan area has about 600,000 people and is heavily industrialized. Oil and gas companies are prominent. It is the northernmost port on the Mississippi River that can handle the largest ocean-going ships. During most of the Civil War, Baton Rouge was occupied by Union troops.

Comfort Inn did have a nice breakfast with fresh eggs, and I took advantage of it before riding away. I asked Siri how to get back to U.S. 61 and one of us messed it up. I had to stop and ask at a Circle K store where the clerk and a customer both chimed in to get me headed the right way. In fact, all I had to do was keep riding on the same street, then take an overpass and ramp to find my favorite road for the last time. I anticipated going all the way to New Orleans on the road that had been very good to me.

Things were about to turn sour. Just as I pedaled onto U.S. 61, the same customer from Circle K came by tooting his horn and waving. He even yelled, "You're going right." I was happy and ready to count down the miles after only adding one mile on the misdirection. Rain was expected again, but later in the day.

Saturday morning traffic was heavy as I pedaled through Prairieville, St. Gabriel and Gonzalez. Louisiana's part of

U.S. 61 was pitted and often had no shoulder. Then it got worse. The road in the lane wasn't much better than riding in the grass because of all the holes and bad pavement. I began to notice lots of metal on the road including screws, nails, various slivers and the wires from steel belted tires. I had never seen anything like this in all the rest of my bike travels. I knew at that point that I would be very lucky to finish the ride to New Orleans without a flat. I didn't have one so far on the rest of the trip, but no other roads had this kind of trash. I usually wear my glasses on the road so that I have a better chance to see metal and I search for it constantly. Obviously, Louisiana did not clean their roads like other states do, either with a vacuum truck, a blower or a spinning brush. When there was no shoulder to ride, chances were more likely the metal would cause a flat. When there was a shoulder, I rode in the place that had less metal. More glass began to show up too. I just kept pedaling.

Most of the scenery by midday was just woods and an occasional house. Not much else. I noticed the storm clouds building fast and the wind began to pick up. I needed a store or some type of overhang because this storm looked serious. In another God moment, Stump's convenience store appeared just as the first few drops fell and the wind became a gale. Within a hundred yards of the store, my blue and black running hat blew off. I immediately stopped to look for it, but I couldn't find it. With the downpour started, I jumped back on the bike and got under the overhang at the side of the store.

With enough time to wait out the worst of the storm, I visited with Ann and her staff in the store. We had a nice conversation with everyone involved. No customers came in for half an hour. As the worst of the wind and rain decreased in intensity, I pedaled on expecting to ride in rain for a while based on the heavy cloud cover.

After about 45 miles for the day, I realized that a small thumping was coming from the back tire. It was the sound of a coming flat and the tire began to deflate. My average over all of the bicycle adventures had been one flat about every 1,000 miles, way better than most people do. For the last few years, I have ridden on puncture-resistant tires. I was well past the 1,000-mile distance on this trip and was due for one, especially with all the metal on the roads. The rain was steady, and I had no good place to work on the tire. I found a short gravel pullout and stopped there.

It's a big deal to repair a rear tire. First the panniers have to be taken off the bike, although I often lay the bike on one of them. I drop the tire from the frame by loosening the spin-tighteners that hold the axle in place. Next comes taking the chain off the derailleur and gears to allow the tire to be removed. The tire was very flat, so I slid the tire to one side of the rim and pulled the tube out. I found the cut in the tube and decided to replace it. I never patch a tube because the patch is hard to seal correctly, and the tube is likely worn anyway. Instead, I use a new tube to replace the bad one. Often, the reason for the flat is still in the tire so I take time to run my fingers all around the inside of the tire. Then I visually inspect the outside of the tire as a precaution. Anything I find, I make sure to get it out. I had two tubes left after this repair.

I found the newly inserted tube wouldn't hold air and was likely defective. I took the tube out and replaced it with another. After hooking everything back up, it wasn't long before I had yet another flat. Tired and wet, I was glad to see a motorcycle with a trailer and then a pickup truck both pull in to help. Johnny Walker was touring from Florida on his motorcycle and David Bourg was on his way home. Both were great guys and jumped in to help me put in the last tube I had. We did all the steps again and were confident that the tube and tire would hold air.

At this point, the day was getting away from me. With the cloudy and rainy afternoon, I was now unlikely to still have time to make the last 35 miles to New Orleans. David gave me his card and offered to help if anything else happened. I pedaled away and everything was fine for about five miles. As you probably expect by this time, my tire went flat again. I was just down the road from another convenience store and went there. Without another tube and no time or way to get another, I contacted Uber to see about a possible ride. There were no vehicles available that were big enough to haul the bike.

While I was waiting for Uber, I sat inside a freezing convenience store. The restaurant part had closed for the evening, and I was out of options. I didn't even have my sleeping bag after sending it back home the day before. I reluctantly called David Bourg back, hoping that he was still good to help me once again. David answered and told me that he had committed to doing a project the rest of evening for his wife. David then said that he would talk to her and call me back. I watched people come and go and wondered if any of them would be interested in hauling me and the bike to downtown New Orleans, now 30 miles away.

David called back and said he would come get me. I was pretty down at this point because I had never failed to finish a particular adventure on the bike. Those 30 miles were haunting me. I had a free day planned for visiting the city on Sunday and tried to figure a way to get back out and ride that 30 miles before returning to New Orleans for the train ride home on Monday.

Bicycle shops don't open early, particularly on Sunday, and there was a good chance another flat or two would happen. I brooded a little while waiting for David to drive the 12 miles from his home. The familiar red truck drove into the parking lot, and we loaded the bike and gear.

What followed was a wonderful conversation that I will never forget. David works for Valero in refinery planning, and we shared thoughts about our families and work histories, plus what mattered most to us. Next came life lessons learned and how we should do as much as possible for oth-

RIVER RIDE

ers. David said, "I told my wife that I needed to come help you out." But most memorable were his words about "paying it forward" and how he had come to honor and serve this phrase. "Paying it forward" was exactly what he did on this night, and of course he wouldn't take any money. We stood in the dark across from the hotel, took a few pictures and continued to talk. My mood was sky-high after the ride and discussion as we shared three hugs, several photos and four handshakes. I hated to see David go, but it was already approaching 8 p.m. and he was still close to an hour from home. He was part of at least two "God moments" in the same day!

I took the bike and walked across the street to an upscale high-rise Best Western. I waited for the front door to be unlocked, an odd occurrence. I walked in and the desk clerk and a sort of doorman both looked at me as I rolled the bike into the lobby. The inevitable next hiccup came when the front desk person told me that my reservation was for the next night. I told her that it was supposed to be for both nights and that I planned to leave by train early on Monday morning. After hitting a bunch of keys, she told me that I definitely didn't have a reservation, but she could go ahead and book me for the evening. At a higher rate of course.

I took the room and asked for the elevator. The doorman stepped in and took my bike, still with the flat tire. I told him that I had been assured that I could keep the bike in my room, which I had. In his practiced and aloof sort of way, the doorman told me that no one ever got to keep a bike in the room there. He showed me where it would be parked, and then gave me a claim ticket with which I could get it at any time. Remember this as the tale develops.

Shortly afterward, I was secure in my room with old brick walls and one good view. I put my bags down and resolved to eat what I still had in the bags rather than going out any more for the evening. I had also been assured that I could get a full breakfast the next morning. My brain was worn out and I needed a shower, so I planned to watch a little TV, eat some cookies and crackers and get a good night's sleep.

I settled in bed and realized that from somewhere there was a loud motor running. I figured out that the motor noises were coming from the air conditioning and wondered if I could just shut it off. I did but woke up a couple hours later with the room progressively getting warmer. This was a warm summer night after a very humid day. The warmth wasn't going away unless I turned the unit back on and then I would have the motor to listen to. Fifty-one miles today seemed long ago as I set the thermostat at a slightly cooler temperature and went back to bed.

Up early the next morning, sightseeing was on my mind. I couldn't wait to see the World War II Museum, currently rated as New Orleans' top tourist attraction. Having visited the city about 15 years before, I had memories both good and bad and hoped for new ones this time. I walked just over half a mile to the museum, arrived a little early and decided to walk around the outside where several statues waited patiently. A few other folks were out walking too, most of them headed the same direction as I was. I went to a little courtyard and sat down briefly outside from where I could see the entrance. I then noticed a life-sized statue of Anne Frank and found it very moving to look into her face. Just a few short steps away was a group of statues dressed in flight suits. Most were bronze, but a few in gray signified the airmen who were at yesterday's briefing but didn't return. All of this set the tone for what I hoped to see inside.

The morning had been quiet as I waited for the doors to open at 9 a.m. Suddenly I heard a large man shouting in the street at the next intersection. Quite overweight, he had his belly out for all to see as he hollered at each car that passed. Then he started making threatening gestures. I turned away to watch the door as people started to go inside the museum. Just as I got in line, the large man walked by while carrying on an enthusiastic conversation with himself.

Inside the door of the museum, I found myself in a huge open area with planes and weapons overhead. Everyone got to choose whether to pay just the admission or to add Tom Hanks' movie to the experience. I, of course, chose both. Each person who entered was loaded on a simulated troop train for a brief welcome and assigned a special participant in WWII with a QR code where we could load information throughout the museum on his or her exploits. Ahead were endless galleries related to a portion of the war. The United

States was first shown with an undersized and ill-prepared armed forces ramping up to take on the two most powerful military machines ever seen.

Historian and author Stephen Ambrose, along with movie producer Stephen Spielberg, got credit for starting the museum. Hanks and many others joined in. I had a 10 a.m. movie ticket and took in all I could of the first galleries before the movie, quickly finding an almost endless relating of how the boy and girl next door went to war. Recordings and photos of the brave who survived were just around every corner, with many Medal of Honor recipients described. Most moving were the recordings of those who lived to receive America's greatest medal, but then were killed later in the war. I knew already why this museum was rated as New Orleans' best attraction.

I changed buildings to see Hanks' movie, my first in 4D and complete with moving chairs and floors, with speakers all around. The movie was a depiction of how America was thrust into the war and ultimately able to win due to a never before seen commitment from its citizens. I stayed for five hours and could easily have stayed for more than a day. I think I remember that each ticket was good for two days' admission.

Outside, I looked for a quick snack as I got my bearings and moved toward the river. Traffic was light and walking was easy. I stopped at a little bakery and made my first interesting purchase. A large cookie and a bottle of water

RIVER RIDE

were $5 and $3, which immediately made me think I must be in an airport or at a Major League baseball game. While eating I walked back toward my motel and noticed a small pizza store. Finding prices more to my liking, I got two huge slices and more water, and told them I would likely be back.

The river and Jackson Square were just ahead. With a wonderful viewing area of the river, I sat on a bench for the first of several times during the day. Various boats and ships came by and some sort of entertainment was easy to find, although a lot less than I remembered from my past visit. Jackson Square, honoring Andrew Jackson, is what I consider the center of old New Orleans. On my first visit, Jackson Square was lively with fantastic street performers everywhere. But it was dirty, and the area had not been kept up well. On this visit, Jackson Square was a nice fenced-in park. The performers had moved to the river viewing area, while the open-air vendors had moved to a closed roadway and wide sidewalk just outside the park fence. Lots of retail shops were around.

I watched a sightseeing bus come by and make a stop to drop off and pick up passengers. I checked to find the operation times of the tours and when the bus would be back again, and quickly bought a ticket. Always a huge fan of big city tours by bus, mostly to get my bearings and make a plan of more to see, I went into a CVS for a cold drink and another snack. The next tour bus was due, but I gambled that

I could get what I wanted and get back out in time. Immediately upon entering, I grabbed what I wanted and began waiting in line to checkout. I realized that no registers were running, and everybody had to self-checkout. Not a problem in my case, but those with bigger purchasers slowed the line. The store staff seemed to keep circulating through the store, making me wonder if theft was the reason for this. Just as I exited, the tour bus pulled up. Yesterday's questionable luck had made a good turn.

The tour was set for 90 minutes, with about 18 stops where passengers could leave and return. However, we were reminded that the buses were nearing the end of the day. The tour leader told us which stops would have another pickup when anyone got up to leave.

My surprise at how much cleaner and brighter New Orleans is now couldn't be measured. The city was beautiful, with a mixture of old and new architecture. I found out that the city is in fact an island, with visitors unable to leave except by plane, boat or bridge. With the likelihood of flooding, insurance remains often higher than the house payment. Celebrities John Goodman and Sandra Bullock have their main residences here. Beyonce had just bought a beautiful old church, nearly a block long. She was intent on making it into a residence. Nicholas Cage owned several residences but was rumored to be in foreclosure due to nonpayment of taxes.

I was most intrigued to be reminded that all burials in

the city must be made above ground. Nicholas Cage also owns several elaborate tombs. The tour leader told us that more than one person could be buried in the same tomb, but not within a year of the previous burial.

The trolley system has tracks at the center of many of the most popular streets. One trolley is 90 years old, and the system has operated since 1835. Most of the cars were beautiful and near full. I walked through a busy downtown market as it was closing and picked up a few things for my daughters and granddaughter. I will admit to a little haggling after one vendor didn't want to let me go without a sale. When he gave in, he acted really exasperated with me. I bought a piece, listed for $50, for $20. I am sure the guy didn't get hurt much on the sale.

A few more highlights of the evening were still ahead, although the day was already a good one. I had been instructed by some female friends to get a beignet, a sort of French pastry loaded with sugar. Some call them donuts, but I messed up the endless line by asking for mine without being coated in powdered sugar. The 24-hour place, within sight of the Andrew Jackson statue, was doing a booming business with two staff members filling orders while the rest made the beignets. The line never stops at Café Du Monde for seven days a week. I got a standard bag of three and did enjoy them. The calories onboard had to be huge, although I never saw anything posted. The café had entertainment; I'm not sure if it was arranged and paid for, or if a street performer had just sat down to eat and sing a little at the same time. I could have stayed to listen.

Just a few steps ahead, I saw a guy selling water and soft drinks out of several huge coolers. Usually wary of scammers, I approached him and said I wanted two of the $2 waters. He had separate coolers with signs that said $2 on one and $3 on the other. He pulled them out of an unlabeled cooler and said, "That will be $5." I am sure that he didn't realize that I had just ridden 20 days on a bike with plenty of time to do math problems. I quickly replied, "I want two of the $2 waters." Then I handed him $4, and he reached into yet another cooler and handed me the bottles of water, then said, "You get it at a discount!"

I walked back to the river's observation area and ate a couple of the beignets while drinking my special water. A street performer with a keyboard was taking requests. He sang well. I noticed that no one seemed to be giving him any money, and he soon announced that this was in fact the case. Still happy with my water and market purchases, I gave him $5 and began to walk back toward the hotel.

On the sidewalk on the flood levee, I noticed some minor activity where a few people were taking pictures of a gate that appeared to be locked. On the other side of the gate was a short sidewalk to the water. Once closer, I saw the gate was in fact locked by hundreds of padlocks. I watched people walk up and find a tiny piece of the chain link gate and add another lock, while everyone watching smiled and

RIVER RIDE

a few made photos. Yet another new experience. I heard later that the locks signified an everlasting relationship.

One more purchase remained. I went back to the pizza place and got a huge slice and two more bottles of $1.50 water. I called it the best meal in town.

I walked back to the hotel, just a few short blocks away and found the front door unlocked. I checked with the front desk person, a different one, and told her I would be leaving early the next morning for the train ride back to North Carolina. I didn't mention the loud fan but did say that I would need to get my bike and asked if anyone would be available to get it. She replied with a beautiful smile and a very bright, "Yes, there is always someone here who can get it." Remember that too!

I went to my room, rearranged anything that I needed to in my bag, ate the rest of my pizza and fancy French donuts and went to bed with the soothing sounds of a loud fan in an overpriced room. This had still been another wonderful day. I immediately decided that the return trip to New Orleans to ride my last 30 miles into the city would come soon.

The last chapter of Part I will recount my travels home, leaving New Orleans behind for just a while.

chapter 7

Amtrak and the ride home

Today had a lot of promise. I was up especially early, mostly because I knew I could sleep on the train home. My second Best Western night was pleasant, especially because I didn't notice the noise from the loud fan as much. The room was nice otherwise, but I was ready to go home.

Two things were on my mind before I left the hotel. I wanted to see if I could grab some breakfast a little early. The breakfast was good yesterday but was slow to evolve. Supposed to be ready at 7, only a few things were in place by then. Lots of people were waiting. I expected the same today, but I noticed a pan of bagels already on the counter. I grabbed a couple and decided to eat them on the way to the station, just before the breakfast person told me that the meal was not yet open. I told him I had a train to catch and that I was walking, especially since I wasn't going to put the bagels back. I left the breakfast area with those bagels and headed to the front office to ask for my bike. Remember that the front desk person told me already that someone would always be there to get me the bike. I had my ticket.

The woman I found at the front desk was new to me, but

very pleasant. I handed her my ticket and told her that I was walking to the train station. She offered to print me off walking directions, but I told her I was pretty sure where it was and had it on my phone. Then she went out and started to look for my bike. There were several rooms off the lobby. After she went to a second incorrect one, I told her that I knew where it was and would be glad to get it. She said, "No one is allowed back there." I replied, "Well, I went back there and parked it when I checked in." I walked right behind her to where the bike was and got it myself to roll out, after we both moved some things out of the way.

I left the hotel and ate a bagel as I walked the bike along the sidewalk. I had plenty of time to get to the train station, flat tire or not. The tires are good enough that I couldn't tell the tire was flat when not on the seat. A quick 1.1 miles and I was inside the terminal. They had a policeman who appeared to be directing people to where they needed to go. I told him that I was going home on the train, and he said, "Taking the bike?" I said, "Yes, it's on my ticket."

I had not ridden a long train journey since a trip to New York City about 20 years ago when we got on that train in the super early morning at Salisbury. It was the very same train that I would ride home for the next 20-plus hours. Now called the Crescent, I am pretty sure it used to be called the Southern Crescent. The Crescent was parked right outside the doors, along with another train that was going west.

RIVER RIDE

One of my former running clients has long been my travel agent for these adventures. Remember Allison Tuck, owner of Travels by Allison, from earlier in the book? We've had some big wins on my adventures and things have always worked out. I mention that because I walked the bike to the desk, complete with the bags still hanging on it. I had a ticket that stated that the train would take me and the bike to Salisbury.

That was not good enough according to Cheryl Linyear, the head ticket agent. This was a new issue to me. I thought if I had a ticket and the ticket said that we both could ride the train, then I was set. Cheryl looked at some things on her screen and said that there was no baggage agent in Salisbury, therefore the bike couldn't go because no one was there to take it off the train. I told her I didn't have any other way to get the bike home. Cheryl talked to someone on the phone who said, "It says the bike can go on the ticket, doesn't it? Then the bike can go." The train staff will have to help get it out of the baggage car. Cheryl smiled and asked about my ride, pleasantly going about her work and then handed me a paper that showed my positive status to get home. She took the bike and rolled it into the back of the terminal. I didn't see it again until we stopped in Salisbury. I kept my bags and decided to fill the next hour by grabbing breakfast at the Subway in the terminal while answering some messages. The terminal was filling quickly since both trains would leave at about the same time. Mine was set to board at 8:45 a.m. and we should leave about 9:15. I was pumped and looking forward to the long journey.

Travel agent Allison had booked the train trip. While we were talking about it, she mentioned her own recent trip on Amtrak using a roomette. I hadn't heard of a roomette, but Allison described it as my own little piece of heaven, a very quiet small room with great seats, a big window, my own thermostat, sink and toilet. A shower was available elsewhere on the car, but I didn't anticipate needing it.

While waiting for boarding, I grabbed some extra Subway cookies and a drink. I already had a few things in my bag, and some water and a dining car were available on the train. We began boarding, but I apparently missed my group and Cheryl told me to just go to the train and get on the front of the third car from the back. I did just that, full of anticipation and ready to get underway. I stepped on the train and met the two guys who apparently would be working in our car. One of them said, "Just turn left and go down the hallway." I did that but somehow walked directly into a full bedroom. One of the train guys quickly said, "No, farther down the hall!"

I found my roomette, number 9, just what I expected and just about perfect. One of the train guys stopped by and told me about the roomette and that we would be leaving in about 10 minutes. I put my bags on the other seat and looked around. I could see the roomette across the hallway, but we both had curtains. A few others passed by and then

RIVER RIDE

the head train guy stopped in for a few instructions. He told me not to use the toilet without flushing or we would both be unhappy. The dining car was available but be aware that it would likely be very busy. One of the staff would be by early in the evening to set up my bed. And finally, they would be by to take my meal order once the train was underway. A lot to take in, and I wasn't sure what he meant about my meal order.

An hour or so later, the head car guy stopped in and told me lunch orders were being taken. He gave me a menu with vegetarian options, and I chose one. No prices were listed, and I figured to just go with it and see what happened. I was texting and emailing to answer questions, plus watching the scenery fly by. We had 18 stops planned, so a little less than one an hour. It was pleasant to hear the conductor come over the speakers and tell us about the stops ahead and how the train was doing on its schedule. With rain again falling outside, I was more comfortable and relaxed than I had been in close to a month. My first nap came about this time.

Other favorite parts of the train ride included the horn and its sound in my car as we approached crossings. I was amazed at how peaceful and quiet the whole experience was. I started writing my ending to the Mississippi River adventure Part I for the Post, and occasionally nodded off.

My lunch came and it was wonderfully done, very tasty. The train guy took my order for the evening meal, another veggie option. I thought maybe they were going to bill my card for the meals, but that evening I was informed by the travel agent that all meals are included. Could this whole thing get any better?

Still raining and cloudy through the evening, the train was ahead of schedule and made several stops where passengers could get off and walk around for 10 minutes. Those stops included the only conversations I had with anyone other than the train staff.

About 7 p.m., both of the car guys came by to fix my bed. New to this, I said, "Sure, just do what you think is best." They asked if I wanted to sleep overhead or down below. I asked, "What do most people do?" They suggested making a bed from the seats below and they did it. The bed took up most of the available floor room.

I did talk to the guy across the hall who makes the trip from New Orleans to New York City once a week. He told me that I might be more comfortable during the night if they just reclined one of the seats and I slept that way. I quickly realized that he had a good point. In the bed, I felt the swaying of the train more, which every so often pitched me to one side or the other. I hadn't noticed that during the day. Later I found out that overhead bed is even more likely to do this.

For most of the day, I had hoped to get the Yankees game on my iPad during the evening. Since we were rolling fast, the WiFi sometimes went out and then would suddenly

RIVER RIDE

reconnect. I connected to the game and was able to listen to about 75% of it. By then, the sky was dark with scenery only available when we passed through towns. Darkness would still prevail when we arrived back in Salisbury.

My sleep wasn't the best because of the swaying of the cars, but the hallway was dark, and the conductor had stopped announcing upcoming stops. All those about to get off were notified by a quiet visit from the car staff.

The Crescent made it back to Salisbury a few minutes ahead of schedule. I had already been informed that the conductor would go back to the baggage car and hand the bike down to me while I stood on the platform. It worked well, except I immediately noticed that the front wheel was loose. It was probably taken off for storage as we rode. I fixed that and rolled it to the depot as my train experience ended. The Crescent headed on to New York City without me. I quickly realized while I waited for my ride back to the farm that the Salisbury station did have an agent.

I eventually sent Cheryl a thank you message and a couple of books, while telling her that the Salisbury station did in fact have a baggage agent during the times of day when trains stopped.

My daughter and granddaughter took me home. Part I of this two-part adventure was over. A lot of thoughts were and still are rolling around in my mind and I'll take the time to share them.

During the next few days, I couldn't shake the fact that

for the first time I had not completed the end of a ride. I began to think of ways to do it, both as a separate item and possibly as a continuation of the plans I was making for the 2023 summer ride. The train ride was so easy and comfortable that I could just load the bike up from here and head for a long weekend in New Orleans that would include the last 30 miles. It still might get done that way, but I am also considering a much longer option.

Over the first month home, I began to realize that to make this Mississippi River ride complete, I had to again ride as close to the river as possible on the way to the source at Lake Itasca State Park. It's about 600 miles north from Dubuque, Iowa. The river past Minneapolis will be much smaller until back at the source, where it is about 12 feet wide and a couple of feet deep.

On my 2017 ride, I saw the source and saw a growing river once more when the river was maybe 30 feet wide. Then I headed east on the way to Green Bay, Wisconsin. I never saw it grow in volume or some of the small towns along the way. Now I want to know the whole river and feel a certain need to do this. I have been reading everything I can find about the river and know much more now than I did during the just completed segment.

So, maps already in hand, that is my plan. I want to return and do a better job on the portion of the river I thought I already knew, but know now that I don't.

And past that, I have an additional challenge in mind.

From Lake Itasca, I plan to ride east about 180 miles to Duluth, Minnesota, and then turn north along Lake Superior. I visited Duluth on that same Northern Tier adventure but turned south. This time I want to go north and possibly ride to Canada. I have the map for this too. I've heard that Minnesota has done a great job to enhance cycling along Lake Superior and U.S. 61. Why am I not surprised that I will see that highway again?

U.S. 61, my friend! Instead of following the mighty Mississippi River, it heads east to follow the largest of the Great Lakes. The distance is about 175 miles to Grand Portage National Monument, which is adjacent to the Canadian border. The monument honors the fur traders of the past. A passenger ferry to Isle Royale runs May to October. The Michigan border comes into the picture and is just a few miles from U.S. 61. Isle Royale National Park is in the remote wilderness of Michigan. It is considered the least visited National Park, and is only accessible by plane or boat. There are no roads. I still bet the park will honor my senior pass.

U.S. 61 continues on into Canada, and the area looks very much like complete wilderness. I will continue to research the options. Also, there is a train option from Duluth to New Orleans, and the opportunity to get that last 30 miles. The doors are still open as to how it will all play out.

At present, riding will begin in about five months from this writing, probably in late July. There is just something special to me about riding along the water. I can't wait to get started. I will get the bike ready, probably including ordering some new tires although the ones on it don't look worn. There is equipment to repair. I will try to stay in shape with my running and farm work, and make that farm schedule fit with being gone for maybe about another month.

I find a freedom and certain excitement uncommon to the rest of my life while on that bike and with a destination ahead. As always, I hope the readers will ride along. I am amazed at the knowledge those readers have of almost any area I consider for travel, and please remember that I still haven't been everywhere, but it is on my list!

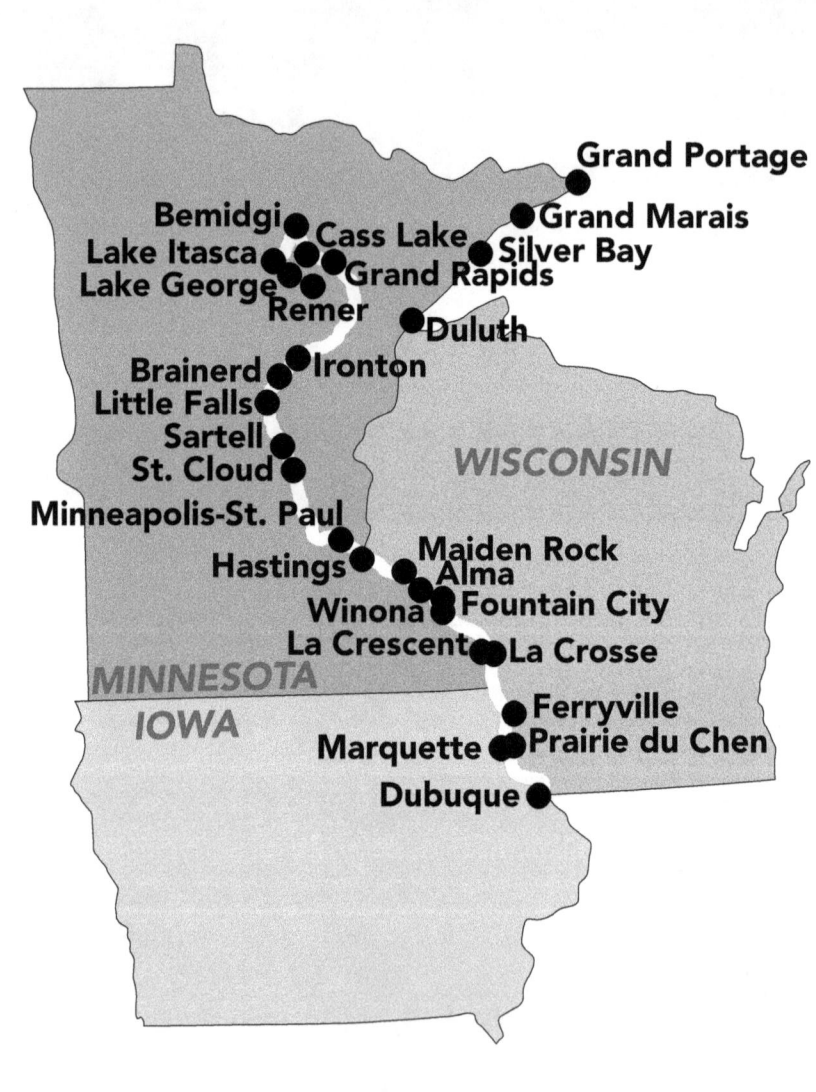

PART II

chapter 8

Dubuque to Minneapolis

I am now exactly one week removed from the day's ride that ended the second part of this book, brought me back to the St. Paul-Minneapolis area and left me more than humbled at the ability to still pull out a century-plus ride when I desperately needed one. I was in a bind, knowing that I had to pick up a one-way rental car on Sunday morning at the airport and begin the nearly 1,300-mile journey home with the bike. Due to serious weather on Friday, I got off the road in the afternoon during rain, lightning and anticipation of more near Barnum, Minnesota. The extreme weather never happened to me, but others got hammered with big hail and damaging winds.

I can reflect now on all of Part II and if it met my expectations for the summer 2023 bike journey. We can now look back and see what happened, what didn't and how I am somewhat better for having completed Part II.

Before the 2022 cycling adventure, I knew certain things about the Mississippi River and gathered some amazing knowledge just ahead of that ride. I had a few things specifically in mind but was open to plan for what seemed the best way to complete the river. By starting in Dubuque and riding south, I got plenty of great views of the wide river. You have already read about those in Part I.

I chose to drive again to Dubuque, Iowa, and not spend much time there since I knew quite a bit from last year. I got that wonderful heads-up at the visitor center and my first ever Great River Road map. I visited the Field of Dreams movie site, made a good afternoon out of sightseeing in Duluth and headed south for all of Part I.

My plan was to drive very close to the same route, return to Dubuque and stop at the visitor center again with an eye toward going north. Two differences stood out this year: one, I made much better time without seeing any major construction, and two, I chose the worst motel of my Mississippi River experience as the stopping off point for the driving portion.

As usual, I started searching the internet for an affordable place as the sun began dropping quickly in the sky. Indianapolis was coming up and Siri's top choice each time was the Gateway Motel, saying that the motel was only one minute off my intended route. I called and the rate was good, especially for a later arrival compared to several other overpriced chains in the same area.

I went to the front desk, and all seemed normal. I got a key to the room and found it lacking a chair and much of a cleanup from the previous resident. The bathroom was especially bad. The pillows were small and very flat. I went back to the office and told her that this was unacceptable.

I was also told that she personally would clean the room while I went out to get something to eat.

Gone long enough to get a Subway sandwich, I was then told that they were sorry, and I had been changed to another room two doors down. I looked in and found no towels, the room only marginally cleaned and still no chair. The sheets, thankfully, did appear to be clean this time. Unable to get the TV to work and not wanting to sit on the bed, I told her I needed a chair. She said, "I will get you one, but we are remodeling all the rooms and the chairs have been sent away."

Back to the room I went and ate my sandwich while listening to a ball game on my iPad. No chair came, but things were quiet. Until…a couple arrived and shortly later some amorous activities began that ended with a terrific pounding against the wall. I gave up, promised myself to be gone by 6 a.m., and went back to sleep. They left before I did, and no other cars arrived during the night. My newest adventure was off to an exasperating start.

Back on the road, I headed for Dubuque again and a plan started to form. While making such good time, I would complete the 1,000-mile drive by just after noon. I had already googled the visitor center and found that it was closed. My Great River Road map was in hand and easy to follow going north. I decided to turn the car in at the airport upon arrival, get on the bike and start riding, therefore gaining a half day.

Siri supplied the shortest route from the airport to Guttenberg, the first town where I could get a motel room. I think she sent me on a hillier route that was a few miles longer than I would have pedaled had I gone directly through Dubuque. I passed through New Vienna and Luxembourg, both small towns, but the scenery was dominated by huge churches at the highest points. Occasionally I would ask for cycling directions, usually with Siri wanting to follow a bunch of turns and get on bike paths and a slightly longer route. Cycling routes also get an elevation profile, but they aren't always correct.

The last hill coming into Guttenberg was very serious and steep, reminding me quickly of Iowa from last summer, but oddly Siri left it out of the elevation profile. I began to see signs referring to local honey for sale just ahead at the scenic overlook. Carol O'Brien had samples of her different varieties of honey and was just setting up her regular spot when I saw her and the overlook. I got my first view of the Mississippi this summer and then talked to Carol. She was nice enough to give me a small bottle of wildflower honey, one that I was amazed to find was quite heavy, usually a no-no for space in my bike bags. Yet I took that wonderful honey and swallowed some each morning of my ride. A week after completion, I still have a very small portion remaining. From my knowledge of honey, local honey is better for a person, but I didn't care that this bottle was local to Iowa. Wildflower honey tasted great, and I used it for added energy.

I pedaled into Guttenberg after leaving several messages at the Guttenberg Motel. Patty Schwarz had told me she would have a room and to let her know for sure if I was coming. I got to the motel, a very good one that would help me forget the Gateway Motel experience. The first few days of the trip were hot, this one in the low 90s. Thankfully the Guttenberg Motel did have a small air conditioning unit. Patty finally called and said my key was in the office and to go on in and we could settle up later.

After unloading part of my pannier weight, I headed to the historic waterfront. Main Street is next to the river, so close that basements do occasionally flood in the area. Guttenberg surprised me with its beauty, but evidently it was well-known nationally. An old German town, Guttenberg was voted America's Rivertown of the Year last year. It has also been named 8 times as one of America's top 25 prettiest towns. The annual Germanfest celebration has been rated as one of the 20 best small-town festivals in the nation.

In beginning Part II, I quickly became immersed in a highly performing convenience store challenge. Kwik Star was the spot for ready-to-eat food, per Patty, who just happened to be the Chamber of Commerce president. I got a F'real Milkshake and some other things, rode back to the river's edge, watched the river traffic and looked at some of the old buildings as I ate. A towboat, which is really a push boat, went by with his many barges chained together in front of him.

I felt good, with the feeling that I had stolen a half day of cycling from tomorrow and boosted the whole trip. My legs had to go right to work, but that was OK. About a week is usually the training period for substantial best leg power production, and the hills today would help.

Feeling the normal excitement of a day on the bicycle with a loosely planned agenda, I went out the next morning to the street in light rain. Light rains are friends, especially on warm days, and this one would eventually qualify. I didn't put my raincoat on, as the cooling effect was perfect. I could add the jacket later. Patty told me to just follow the signs at the north end of town and I would be back on the Great River Road. A freight train came into town as I was leaving, making for some great photos.

I found the right road and experienced a heavy but brief thunderstorm as I climbed two gut-busting hills into MacGregor/Marquette. The first house was built in 1837, the same year a ferry service across the Mississippi began, and I knew this town would be special. Patty in Guttenberg told me that some flooding had happened a couple of weeks before, and my first thought when I looked down Main Street was that the same flooding had hit here too.

I slowly rode into town and realized that no traffic was actually getting through. Main Street was dug up from one end to the other. Big concrete pipes were everywhere, and so was plenty of mud. Sidewalks were chained off, but most of the merchants could be reached. I looked around and saw a friendly looking guy going into the post office, then realized that he had entered from a back road. I stood, slightly bewildered, needing information.

When Jon Stravers came out, I certainly didn't realize how important to my first few days back on the bike seat he would be. I asked Jon how to get out of town, and from that we ended up emailing and texting a couple times a day over the next week. Jon's pointers included the terrain on either side of the river and which side would be closest and with better views. After he showed me how to get out of town through the endless construction, Jon also told me to cross over to Wisconsin for better riding. He said, "You can see the river most of the rest of today and you won't have to ride those endless hills."

The hills didn't go away but they were more reasonable. I passed through Prairie du Chien, then Ferryville and DeSoto. Convenience stores were full of people getting cold drinks, and I was right with them.

With the heat, I was ready to find a place for the evening. I saw a motel listed in Stoddard, Wisconsin and was surprised when they had a room rate of only $70. I wondered if the Water's Edge Motel really was on the water and facing it. I was told to get some food at the Kwik Trip, on the way down to the water. Without enough room in my bags at this point, I could see the water and knew the ride wouldn't be far to the store. Throughout Part II, I heard very high motel prices quite often. Some of it was driven by full or near-full motels, but Water's Edge did confirm my rate at $70 per person. Somehow later when my confirmation came, the charge was $80. My room was obviously meant for at least three people so I couldn't complain. I had a nice futon, three beds, a nice kitchen and an oversized bathroom. Plus, the view of the Mississippi and the dock space had to be worth something.

The motel was totally quiet when I arrived and I put one bag in my room along with the contents of the other, which left me plenty of room for food. I did ride to the Kwik Trip and got ice cream and plenty of food. I was burning big calories and the large convenience stores always had some buys. Bananas were 49 cents a pound instead of a dollar apiece like last year.

I came back to the room and ate while writing. Just before dark, a group of teenage boys came in on a boat and started running through the place. They ended up in the room over my head, were loud and getting louder. I found the dad and asked him to calm them down. He did, and the rest of the evening went well, complete with sunset photos. Trains ran during the night on tracks behind the motel, which suited me just fine. I had 73 miles for this day.

One of my quirky things to do after spending almost any evening in a motel is to clean up behind myself, so much that the room looks nearly as good as when I arrived. I even put my trash in the convenience store bags and don't use the trash cans, so those bags don't have to be replaced. I have done this since my very first trip in 2011. I often wonder what the cleaning people think when they open the door the first time, maybe, "Did he not stay here?"

Jon responded to my questions about which side of the river should come next and suggested crossing back to Minnesota. Up and out ahead of other motel guests, I was stopped by a local driver in his truck on the way to work. He wanted to know where I was from and where I was going. After the N.C., Dubuque, Mississippi River explanation, he told me that I was headed toward oppressive, wind-aided smoke and might want to consider changing my route. I told him that I was committed to Lake Superior regardless, and that we had smoky haze on occasion back in N.C. from Canadian fires. He was surprised at that.

With the heat building, I called ahead to a possible motel for the next evening and it's a good thing I did. I had an even hotter day coming and it was supposed to be windy. I rode to La Cross, Wisconsin, a town of about 51,000 residents. Traffic was busy in the morning. Car lanes disappeared often, pushing me onto the sidewalk. More than that, I began to find endless construction. Jokes and statements concluded that these northern states had only two seasons, five months of road construction and seven months of winter. These states do have bitter cold and roads get rough with pavement buckling, much like what happens on the way through the Yukon and Alaska. Pavement is taken up, leaving gravel and dirt, very unstable for my bike. Much more about this later.

I rode into La Crosse and realized that most of the main thoroughfare would either be closed or partially closed through the town. I decided to just keep riding through the construction as long as possible while using sidewalks where it helped. Workers were all around, but none seemed to care about the loaded bike.

Jon told me to use the Route 14 bridge, the only one that bikes could cross back over the river into Minnesota. The bridge was a beautiful, older one, with both a bike lane on the pavement and a pedestrian lane behind a concrete wall. I noticed one young kid who handled it all like a pro as he led me across to Minnesota.

Over the years, I have mentioned finding money along the road. The biggest amount collected was during my run across North Carolina, but only coins. Never have I even seen any paper money on the road. I have found two wallets with bills, but no loose folding money. Just as I came off the bridge, I noticed a $5 bill flapping in the breeze. I still have that same $5 bill, unsure of how it would have been left behind. While riding, I do keep an eye ever alert to watch for all the sharp things that can cause flats, another concern along the way of every ride. For once, luck came my way. On second thought, luck and answered prayers happen nearly every day.

My intended spot for the night caused me to cross back

over the Mississippi again to Wisconsin. The Hillcrest Motel was owned by a woman who lived in Winona, a spread-out town way ahead of Alma, where I would spend the night. I began to ride on blacktop, or in this case, asphalt that has been sealed with black surfacing. The black repelled the heat and pushed it back up at me. I stopped a couple times for cold iced drinks and began a practice that I had not done before. I bought large drinks with ice in paper cups and stood the cup in one corner of my handlebar bag. The ice seemed to last longer and never once did they spill.

Fountain City was the next town, also very historic. The bank thermometer showed 101 degrees about 3 p.m. in the afternoon. The wind was blowing, but thankfully as a tailwind. My stop at the extremely popular convenience store was timely as everyone else seemed to want a cold drink. The parking lot was jammed. About a dozen teens sat on the sidewalk in a shady spot next to the store while they enjoyed their drinks. I suspect that the temperature was about 96 or 97, instead of 100 plus, but still easily the hottest day of Part II.

The next town was Alma, big for a town in this area and full of historic buildings. I only knew that my room for the evening was on the other side of town, headed north, at the Hillcrest Motel. I was advised again to stop at Kwik Trip and get some food, but the owner also said that I was welcome to use the community kitchen at the motel. I asked Siri to guide me to the motel and she couldn't do it. After asking directions twice, I found I had to ride north until I saw it. Less than a mile out of town, I found the quaint motel with a key already in my door waiting for me. I went in and turned the miniature AC unit on and hoped it would eventually catch up. The room was hot at that time!

I did the same food space unload of my bags and headed back to Kwik Trip. The ride back was into a strong wind and uphill, easy enough to do because I would have the wind and downhill with me while returning.

Once back at the motel, I found that a group of fishermen had nearly the whole place rented. I met many of them and explained over and over what I was doing. The evening cooled dramatically, and while I sat outside writing and eating, then alternately watching trains going by and the setting sun. My view of the Mississippi was part of a turn the great river was making. A sort of bay had formed in front of the motel.

Alma looked much like an old west town and officially became a village in 1868, but immigrants began gathering 20 years before. Riverboat pilots knew the area as 12 Mile Bluff because of a prominent rocky point that could be seen 12 miles away on the river.

I began to encounter increasing drought issues as I headed north. Besides the heat, little rain had fallen in the area recently, but rain was predicted that night. Clouds built strongly to the north before darkness came, but no rain fell. Even without the rain, this was a very relaxing evening as

I watched nature and the trains continue their show until dark. The room was very comfortable, and cooler temperatures were predicted for morning.

The area is also known as a major bald eagle habitat. I saw one as I left the motel the next morning. The eagle dipped into a marshy area, but I don't think it came up with anything. I saw it land again in the top of a dead tree.

When I stopped at a convenience store in Nelson, Wisconsin, the next morning, I asked the clerk two questions. I needed a certain round battery for my cyclometer, but she didn't carry it. Since I had not heard from Jon, I asked her what the scenery was like on the Wisconsin side. She assured me I would see much of the river, long stretches in fact.

I usually listen to a local radio station of some type while riding the bike for extended periods in the rural areas. Bluff Radio was the most dominant station the previous day with awesome legends of country music. Not once did it cross my mind that Bluff Radio was named for anything. I soon found out why the name mattered.

Long hills, many overlooking the river, came and went, over and over. Most of the uphill riding was done in the lowest gears. I had promised myself to stay in the second ring, or series of nine middle gears for the whole ride. A few of these bluffs made me think of shifting to the lower ring and granny gears, but I did not. I constantly looked across the river and didn't see the same bluffs, or at least not as frequently, but I do suspect the bluffs were across the river too because the radio station was.

In what wouldn't be the last historical surprise for this bike adventure, I pedaled into Pepin, on a hill above and right along the river. A big sign declared Pepin as the birthplace of Laura Ingalls Wilder, renowned author of the "Little House on the Prairie" books. A museum about Wilder was also seen.

Two small towns of less than 300 residents were Stockholm and Maiden Rock. A historical marker told the story of the actual maiden rock, where a young Indian maiden was forced into a marriage chosen for her by others. That night she jumped to her death from the rock along what would become the Great River Road. A similar story is part of the Hannibal, Missouri, bus tour. In that situation, the young maiden and her boyfriend jumped together to their deaths since they could not marry as members of opposing tribes.

Near Maiden Rock, I met several members of a motorcycle group who walked over and asked about my ride. Usually the guys on the big motorcycles don't pay a lot of attention to bike riders. But these three seemed genuinely interested in my journey, especially as one of them told about his own journey on a skateboard from Virginia to Wisconsin. He said as I began to ride away, "We have to stay on the move!" I rode the toughest of the bluffs right after that and hoped the motorcycle guys wouldn't see me struggling. We were

RIVER RIDE

all on U.S. 35, but they must have ridden the other way.

The upcoming afternoon and evening had some uncertainty. Big storms were forecast and my best chance of grabbing a room was back over in Minnesota. I crossed over the river, just before Hager City and rode about four miles into the historical city of Red Wing. I hoped the change back to Minnesota would help with the continuous bluffs, but it didn't work. A huge two-mile climb took me over the meanest bluff yet. Red Wing looked interesting, and I hope some day to return for a visit. There were lots of old buildings and several famous shoe factories.

For now, I was back on U.S. 61 and made a right turn toward Hastings, which surprisingly became flat quickly. I grabbed a motel room. Huge clouds were building as I pedaled next door to the Kwik Trip for food. Oddly, the big three of convenience stores, Kwik Trip, Holiday and M&H, were only separated by the motel. By the time I came out of the store, steady rain was falling. I tried a shortcut through a fence that didn't work out and pedaled on into the heavier rain. Rain was pounding down as I found my door. Leading to a hallway, my first door was tight to get in with the bike. A lot of northern motels have an outer door and hallway, before another door enters the actual room.

Rain continued as I began to write and eat in the normal routine. The desk clerk had already told me that the best views of the Mississippi were on the northern edge of town. Once the rain ended and a beautiful rainbow spread across the sky, I settled into the room and planned to catch the river tomorrow. I had 71 miles for the day.

Strawberry ice cream was my choice of the evening, A lifetime, unlimited ice cream sponsorship still exists with the Y Service Club at the South Rowan YMCA, and I am sure they would be disappointed if I did not use it nightly. That is what the readers expected.

Up early the next morning, I wanted to get those photos of the river while leaving Hastings. Minneapolis and St. Paul were ahead. I wore a long-sleeve shirt, as the morning was in the 50s. A cool north wind should boost the day, as should seeing and visiting with Ethan Horne, a long-time friend from back home in China Grove.

I first met Ethan when he played for me on a YMCA basketball team for his fifth-grade and sixth-grade years. More on that later. I had to get to the St. Paul Farmer's Market, which soon became a story within itself. I rode on U.S. 61 as the Twin Cities got closer. As best I could tell, U.S. 61 would take me very close to the farmers' market. But when I actually was in sight of St. Paul's downtown, suddenly the exit for U.S. 61 showed as "Closed." I stopped in the bike lane and looked around, unsure of what to do. I saw the barriers ahead and at least a couple guys at the far end of the exit. As I have often done before, I rode right through the barriers and on until I came close to the men.

I told the men that I wanted to meet some friends at the famers market and thought I could do it by using the rest of the closed exit and making a turn that crossed over the top of the interstate where I couldn't ride. The first man told me, "Sure, if you want to, if you can get across all the mud, that road just ahead will get you there."

Starting toward the end of the exit and the mud, I realized it was thick and deep and I could not even push the bike through it. I decided to walk the bike down to the interstate and try to run across it where I could get on the road I wanted. But on that Saturday morning, traffic was just too heavy. Racing across four lanes of interstate on foot and pushing a bike was not the thing to do. So I got on the bike and rode in the right lane to that first exit, followed it onto a downtown street, then turned back on the interstate in the opposite direction. I took the exit I needed and found the direction toward the farmers market and rode that way.

chapter 9

St. Paul, Ethan Horne and on to Itasca

I had called Ethan and he said he would look for me. I saw him and his fiancée Kim Hyatt quickly and we stopped to talk. One of my goals for the trip had been achieved.

As an 11-year-old, Ethan played on a very good YMCA basketball team that I coached, and he had some skills. Ethan could shoot very well, but he always struggled to keep up with the pace of the game. I knew that Ethan could contribute to the team if he just pushed hard enough to be in the play when it mattered. He got better and better, and worked toward being the best he could be. He played again as a sixth grader, getting better each game.

Ethan's body caught up with his skills and he became a very good high school cross country runner. He actually worked with me at the East Rowan YMCA before going off to college. Ethan graduated with a degree in health promotion.

Somewhere along the way, Ethan's brother and his friend decided to ride bikes to Minnesota for a wedding during the wintertime. Ethan asked at the last minute if he could ride along for part of the way. Before reaching Minnesota, the other two guys dropped out and Ethan continued. His journey continued past Minnesota and meeting Kim, on to the west coast. He then rode the western border along the Pacific Ocean, all on a bike that he got at a yard sale.

Next, he turned east to ride what is called the Southern Tier, or mostly along the Southern border. When he reached Florida, Ethan heard that his sister-in-law's birthday party was going to happen in October and he vowed to make it, still on that yard sale bike. He made the reunion with a day to spare.

Later, Ethan served with the Peace Corps for two years in Guinea. Since then, he's been mostly in Minneapolis, where he now works for the burial unit in the VA Cemetery. Kim and Ethan recently rode their bikes to St. Louis, all of that along the Mississippi River.

With all that said, Ethan wanted to ride with me for a portion of my trip. I have never been big on others riding along, but this is the one person who I knew would make it fun. We would enjoy the time catching up with each other. He knew the way out of St. Paul and on through Minneapolis, some on city streets and some on paved trails along the Mississippi River.

Soon after we started north, Ethan and I stopped to see the inside of St. Paul's Basilica, built in 1914. Ethan found a bubble on his back tire and left me for a while to find a bike shop to fix it. He caught back up just as I had found a frustrating predicament.

RIVER RIDE

A train of railroad tank cars, what looked like hundreds of them, had blocked our planned road out of town to the north. On our bikes, we witnessed people in cars searching for any way out. Every intersection we came to was blocked by more tank cars. We tried a couple of ideas, but nothing worked. Finally, we unloaded our bikes and carried them across the back of one of those endless tank cars. We then reloaded the bags and rode away to the north. Three kids told us they had done the same, and the idea seemed right to us.

As the day turned late, we stopped at a convenience store for drinks and to ask a few questions. We needed a nearby town with a reasonable motel. None showed up initially. A customer in the store knew of one in Anoka called the Regency Inn, although the main road connecting us to it was under major construction. Another detour or two through nearby neighborhoods got us to the motel. We grabbed a meal from Kwik Trip, watched a ball game on TV and had plenty of good conversation to complete a relaxing evening after 61 miles for the day.

The AC unit was not working, and it was hot in the room. Nothing cool was coming out of the unit. The desk clerk came to check it out and said that it just had to run a while. Running the unit a while didn't help, and the clerk eventually changed us to another room.

Ethan and I got on our bikes on a clear and almost chilly morning, and I wanted to ride through the town before we left. Ethan was going to ride with me through the morning and then head back to Minneapolis and home.

Anoka had some historic buildings and also the Rum River, which empties into the Mississippi near the town. A 20-mile trail is under construction that includes both rivers.

After leaving town, we rode north on the Great River Road through Dayton, Otsego and into Monticello through some hilly segments and some easier riding too. We saw turkeys, and apples were growing beside the road on a bright Sunday morning that began to cloud up. Ethan decided to turn around at Monticello and offered me a Minnesota state map, which I later found had a $50 contribution to my ride hidden inside. With his own special cycling accomplishments, it was indeed a pleasure to ride with Ethan.

Monticello was incorporated in 1855 on the banks of the Mississippi. The clouds brought some light rain, then a reappearance of the sun with the emergence of a headwind. I rode past the edge of Clearwater and then on into St. Cloud, where I lost the Great River Road. St. Cloud had 51,000 people. I thought the signs were very good except in areas like this, leaving me unsure of the best route. After making a few calls, I thought that the next town was Little Falls and had one motel. The owner told me it was full already and he didn't expect that to change. Little Falls was 35 miles north but Sartell, the actual next town, had an AmericInn. I was not familiar with that chain but began to find them regularly as I continued north.

RIVER RIDE

I called the AmericInn and spoke to a woman on the phone who immediately put me on hold. I stood and held the phone for too long, then eventually hung up and called back. Ileen Antoinette Geisel was so darn personable that I had a hard time being upset with her, especially once she explained that the front desk became very busy all at once. I tried to get a deal, but couldn't swing it, and eventually pedaled toward her motel anyway. I found a quiet, but more expensive motel than I had hoped to use. Ileen made up for part of that. She was so much fun as we talked about my bike rides. The Mississippi had a small set of rapids, one of the few on the whole river, at Sartell. I had a very pleasant evening there, complete with McDonald's vanilla ice cream.

The source of the Mississippi at Lake Itasca was getting closer, and I began to plan the details. Several bridge crossings were ahead and at each one, I expected to see the river getting smaller. Fewer towns are also ahead as the source grew closer. At this point, Lake Itasca looked three days north and west.

I began to long for better cycling days ahead. In the first seven days, the challenges had been significant, and I had not hit my stride yet. Breakfast at the AmericInn was great and any real eggs are always a plus. I was the only one eating and I ate quickly. The first five miles were right along the river and lots of people were out running and walking past nice middle-class houses whose owners lucked out with the great views. I appreciated the flat riding and light traffic. I passed an old dam and paper mill as I left the Sartell area.

The ride to Little Falls was pleasant too, as the morning stayed cool and I enjoyed my long-sleeve shirt. Less traffic and some river sightings were also nice, especially those that brought the river almost to the road. I was surprised that the river had widened again, likely from more water sources.

The terrain remained friendly as the road entered a state park that included the restored boyhood home of Charles Lindbergh, the famous aviator. Famous for his solo flight across the Atlantic, Lindbergh had often lived here in the summer home of his dad, Congressman Charles A. Lindbergh. The home was beautiful, yet there seemed no activity in the area.

Then the town of Little Falls came into view, just ahead of a very strange conversation. I stopped at the only convenience store nearby, ready for a cold drink. The Great River Road signs were usually easy to follow through the small towns. I had come to a main intersection, a crossroads where I expected to continue ahead since there was no signage of any change. I bought a snack and an odd cold drink of some kind, asking the male clerk if the GRR continued on across the main intersection.

What followed was this reply. "No, the Great River Road ends right here beside the store." I said that couldn't be right because I had a map showing it going all the way to Lake Itasca, the source. I asked, "Can I show you my map?"

I brought it in and put it on his counter, to which he replied, "I don't know about that, but the GRR ends right here." Nothing about that made sense, and I decided to follow my senses and ride ahead on the same road. I even laughed that I would find it and call back to the Speedway store and tell him where the next sign was.

Sure enough, less than a mile north, a GRR road sign signaled a right turn. But that led to a worse problem. I began following the signs again at turns and soon came upon Camp Ripley, a National Guard base. The main gate was very impressive, especially for a military base well out in the country. Camp Ripley encloses 53,000 acres and specializes in cold weather training. A frontier fort, used until the 1870s, is still maintained within the camp.

I stopped at a store across from the main gate and got a few things, ready to continue ahead on what had been a great day so far. I rode past the corner of the base, protected by an old military tank, and then followed the signs to an interstate highway. Some states out west of the Mississippi allow bikes on the interstate, including "Share the Road" signs along the shoulder. Not this time, as the first sign on the interstate ramp was for prohibited things, including bicycles.

At first, I wasn't concerned. Often there is a service road nearby. I asked Siri for help and her route seemed good and still would cover about the same distance. Trouble ahead was my first thought as that first road was gravel, very dusty and dry with the drought. I turned on a flat section and rode about a mile without much of an issue. Then a right turn on much looser gravel and dirt was uphill. I had to push the bike to the top since the bike couldn't get traction. At the top, I got back on the bike and coasted downhill with my feet spread out on both sides. My Surly Long Haul Trucker is not made for fluffy dirt and gravel riding. About that time, I realized that Siri's next turn was for a seven-mile road of more gravel and simply impossible to ride.

Just ahead I noticed a white truck parked beside the road and decided to ask the driver for any ideas. Andy Eller works for Steffes Power and was in the area to troubleshoot problems with an irrigation system. He was enjoying his lunch and just happened to be in the right spot for me. Andy had an iPad with a map showing which roads were gravel and the few that were paved. He offered to haul me and the bike to the end of the gravel road and then shared the shortest paved road directions to the Brainerd area. I followed his suggestions and used the rest of the afternoon climbing out of the dry and dusty area.

Just another challenge in the rear-view mirror that had not been expected, but one that now was conquered. I got to Brainerd late in the afternoon, and then on to neighboring Baxter, where a reasonably priced Super Eight was located. Super Eight seems to vary a lot in pricing and quality too, but this one was just right and perfectly located for the next day's start. My legs felt good, especially after 69 moderate

RIVER RIDE

miles for the day and an Original Sundae Ice Cream Cone by Nestle.

Unknowingly, I had ended the day in the perfect jumping off point for the next morning. I began to formulate a new plan. The GRR called for crossing and recrossing the Mississippi multiple times. I was still going to do most of that but wanted to make Grand Rapids for sure by the end of the day. If successful, this ride would be the longest so far on Part II of this adventure.

I had overactive people in the room above me for most of the night, thinking they must be exceeding the limit of people allowed. About this time on the overall journey, I began the habit of not sleeping again once I woke up during the night. Usually, I wake to go to the bathroom or to get some water, then look at the clock and celebrate the time I have left to sleep. On this whole journey, my plan was to be riding as soon as enough daylight would allow motorists to see me and my red rear flashing light. With thoughts of that, returning to sleep usually didn't happen.

The first towns visited were Ironton and Crosby, almost touching each other. Both are very small but are considered Twin Cities. I stopped in Crosby and asked several people if they could tell me where the Mississippi River was. None of them seemed to know, not even the owner of a nice convenience store with homemade donuts. The owner excused herself from the question because she didn't live close by.

Big lakes were scattered everywhere, but my first sight of

the river was north of Crosby. I couldn't believe how small it was at that point. Iron mining was the staple of the local economy, and a beautiful but somewhat haunting mural of iron miners was extremely well done.

I stopped in the small town of Emily to eat a breakfast biscuit that I had saved since Crosby. As soon as I left the crossroads town, the clouds I had watched ahead for the last hour opened up. The conditions for a cyclist became very dangerous, with the heavy rain and low visibility mixed with overdone rumble strips and moderate traffic. I saw a couple of places where I could wait out the storm, but I had a long ride already and no time to waste.

I rode north on Minnesota State Road 6 for 50 miles and dried out well. I didn't stop for more food but did get to pass through Remer again. I had visited Remer on my Northwest Tier ride from Washington to Green Bay, a time when Remer called itself the Bigfoot Capital of the World. In those days, a life-size Bigfoot cutout stood at both entrances to town, and others could be seen through the town. Remer used to be touted as the home of the Bigfoot Olympics. Something was missing this time, a lesser energy of sorts.

Entering the homestretch for the day's ride, I saw yet another storm coming from the north. This one looked serious too, so I stopped to put my raincoat on and confirm a motel ahead in Grand Rapids. I had called earlier and been given a price, but when I called back to book it, the price had gone away. I told the guy on the phone that I was about to be drenched by rain and needed to know. He called back and agreed to the price I was promised.

I rode north through the storm with multiple tractor-trailers appearing to enjoy spraying me. This storm was less intense and didn't last long. I had reserved the room at the end of the ride that involved good tailwinds amid the storms. As I rode into town, I saw my place and realized it was a trendy bar and café with overpriced rooms overhead. Not my type of casual place, but I quickly checked in and got my receipt without paying attention.

I had to carry my bike and bags upstairs, hard enough after 86 miles. Once in my room, I looked at the receipt and realized that I had in fact been charged the higher price. I went to the desk and stayed there until they corrected it, with some help from a management person. The room was OK, nothing special for the price, and thankfully the bar didn't get loud. A Burger King Impossible Burger was my only reward for this from the nearest source of food. No ice cream tonight because I had been wet and somewhat cold for part of the day. Warmer days and more ice cream were ahead.

I was sure I had it all figured out as I got ready to leave Grand Rapids. I didn't rush as much, thinking I had only 70 miles to go and didn't need to be in Bemidji until at least 4:30 p.m. I got breakfast twice and stopped to enjoy eating twice too. I found U.S. 2 very easy to ride with no serious climbing and a wide bike shoulder. I rode through White Oak and Deep River, stopping to eat again. These towns in Minnesota are always clean and there is little roadside trash.

I was about 30 miles into my ride to Bemidji when my running friend and local resident, Michael Zachow, texted me that I must not realize that the Lake George Pines Motel is about 25 miles south of Bemidji, not in it. In a car, that is a little over half an hour. On a loaded bike in hilly terrain, that is about three to four hours. I called the motel, and the owner confirmed his location and gave me his suggestion on the route to take. The good thing is that I would be much closer at the end of the day to Lake Itasca. I decided to make a hard push and get those added miles done as quickly as possible. Sometimes, I can challenge myself on the bike to get more done than seems possible. At first look, I had a realistic expectation of a 7-7:30 p.m. arrival.

Already aware that the town of Lake George had a convenience store, I was not worried about finding food. I had a good price at the Lake George Motel and all I had to do was start pedaling south. I was close to Cass Lake, with several convenience stores, and grabbed a pack of AA batteries, a cold Mountain Dew and Reese's Big Cups. My radio batteries were running out, and the Dew and Reese's were my supercharger. I have actually felt my heart pumping harder right after downing the supercharger combination at other challenging times.

As memory serves, I had to turn off U.S. 2, then take two

very hilly country roads, before joining U.S. 71 all the way to Lake George. Weather was reasonable, I felt strong and there were no towns in route. All I had to do was pedal. Traffic remained moderate and the road shoulder was good on the two main roads. This was an afternoon to enjoy long-distance bike riding.

I stopped after a long climb up to the Lake George Pines Motel, completing the ride before 7:15. I stopped in the motel office, left my things in the wonderful room and headed immediately to the previously mentioned convenience store. A fairly new store, it was busy but had a series of things going against it. I was really hungry after not eating for the afternoon. His stock was limited, prices were high, and he was nearing the 8 p.m. closing time. The only ice cream possibility was half gallons, too much for me. I bought nearly three bags of stuff, including some ice because the motel didn't have it. The clerk said, "Wow, you weren't kidding when you said you would eat a lot!"

A customer in the store asked where I was riding to, and I mentioned Lake Itasca, Duluth and possibly Canada. He was the first of many to say, "Then don't miss Betty's Pies! You will never eat better pie!" I assured him I would stop.

The town of Lake George was listed with 233 residents and inside the Paul Bunyan National Forest. I asked the motel owner about the route to the Lake Itasca Visitor Center, and already had a thick, glossy brochure. The park and visitor center opened at 8 a.m. per the flyer, and I decided to be there at 7:59 to enter the park the next morning. My ride was 85 miles on this day. It was very rewarding to make the destination change and still have time to relax for the evening as I wrote, ate and listened to the Yankees' game. The motel room was clean, quiet and comfortable, with one of the best hot showers of the whole adventure.

I had been to Lake Itasca before, during that same Northern Tier ride. I knew there were some changes made at the park but was sure I could get in at 8 a.m. and spend a couple hours checking things out. I was especially excited to see the source after following the river all the way to New Orleans over the last year.

After a great night's sleep, I rode past the still-closed store and headed into a cool morning and bright sun on the way to the park. I did, in fact, arrive at the park entrance at 7:59 a.m. and coasted up to the gateway building. Closed when I arrived and still closed a few minutes later, I watched the cars drive past. I was supposed to pay a park fee to get in, but no one was there to take it. Two workers were striping the parking lot at the new visitor center. I stopped to ask them what to do, and one of them said, "Summer hours have the park opening at 9 a.m." I asked why the cars were coming on in since there was certainly nothing to stop them. The worker told me that someone would man the entrance at 9 and the other buildings would open at 9 or 10 a.m., again citing summer hours.

I can't imagine how many people visit the park when

the snow is feet deep and the temperatures are well below zero, but those are the times that the park is staffed at a full schedule. All this is very hard for me to understand.

All the serious hills in the park had slipped my mind, as did the five-mile ride to get to the Lake Itasca source. There is a bike trail, but I took the main road and arrived there about 8:45, still with nothing open. Yet the park was filling fast with all those other people who drove right on in. The trail out to the river source, almost considered hallowed ground to me and a bunch of other enthusiasts, was already busy. People were in the water where the trickle was 12 feet wide. They were ready to say, "I walked across the Mississippi River."

Lots of facts and information about the river are still posted outside the gift shop and cafe at the Mary Gibbs Center, neither of which would open until 10. Mary Gibbs was the only female Lake Itasca Park manager. I looked around, made my photos and headed out of the park for the ride to Bemidji into a stout headwind. My Mississippi River ride was now complete, except for a small technicality that will be remedied later this year.

Instead of riding the recognized 2,552 miles of the winding river, I have technically ridden about 2,520. Actual distances that can be ridden along the river vary for several reasons. The river twists and turns constantly, and the distance is different depending on the side of the river. You're right, I am at least 30 miles short. Last August, I had three flats on the last day of my scheduled ride. The bike and I got a truck ride to inner city New Orleans after I ran out of tubes. More on this later as I work out the logistics to finally complete my personal Mississippi River journey.

And lastly for this portion, I wanted to share my recollection of one of the worst parts of all my bike journeys. On my first trip to Lake Itasca Park, I had a flat tire about halfway through the already mentioned five-mile ride. In the early morning, with no breeze and warm temperatures, I was attacked by big flies and massive mosquitoes while I was making the repair. They bit me and I slapped them, making little progress. I decided to take the bites and make the repair quicker. No other tire repair has ever been so miserable.

I was only pursued by one mosquito this time around.

chapter 10

From Lake Itasca to Bemidji and on to Duluth

I missed seeing Bemidji in the proper order on the Great River Road because of my misunderstanding of the location for the Lake George Pine Motel. The proper order to follow the river in reverse back to the source at Lake Itasca Park is to go through Grand Rapids, then Bemidji and on down to the park.

My journey ended up following the river from the source to Bemidji on this portion, following the Great River Road north and east. Seeming uphill, the headwind increased as I followed the forested county roads.

An extra challenge hit me about halfway as I rode towards road construction signs and a gravel road where pavement had been removed. Minnesota is certainly a cold weather area and that cold does major damage to the roads. My memories from the Yukon and Alaska included lots of roads stripped of pavement after the extreme cold and moisture had buckled it. Winter does the damage, and the repairs are done in the summer.

This was a total surprise, but I was well-schooled in what riding on a loaded bike on this surface would be like. As I found near Camp Ripley, the extreme dryness added to the seriousness of the situation. I remember the sign saying 5.6 miles of construction, immediately resigning me to a slow ride and just trying to stay on top of the loaded bike. As I have experienced before, there are portions of the road stripped of more of the shifting gravel. Some parts are still packed a little bit and they are easier to ride, but nothing is consistent. I kept searching for the better-packed spots and tried to ride on them. Another irritant was the construction trucks driving by way too fast and raising a huge dust cloud. Few other vehicles came by.

About midway through, I let the bike get away from me and fell very hard. At some point on such a loose surface, the front wheel starts slipping and sliding sideways and all control is lost. At that point, the cyclist knows they are going down hard. I fell hard to the right, over a little mound of gravel and dirt. Nothing on the bike was hurt as far as I could tell, and I thought too that I was fine. Nothing remained to do but pick up the bike and pedal on, hoping not to repeat the fall.

For a positive, the road seemed to have been watered down on the far end, and regular drivers did not abuse their speed on the road. In Alaska, the roads were so dry that I had to use a T-shirt to filter the dust especially when tractor-trailers with all those tires drove way too fast, spreading maximum dust. Nothing like that was witnessed in Minnesota.

I booked a room at another Super Eight in Bemidji, an

easy one to find and near many food options. Since it was a little more expensive, an evening desk clerk helped me apply all the available discounts to lower the final cost. I enjoy playing the motel game, but sometimes they just aren't willing to talk about a lower price and give me no credit for lots of nights on the road. Still, I was happy with the location of the Super Eight. A wonderful recliner was the headliner of the room. I know not to recline completely unless I have time for a nap.

Shortly after I checked in, it was back to the bike for a ride to the Big River Spoon for ice cream with Michael Zachow who lives in Bemidji. I met Michael in Salisbury, N.C., this past February when he came all the way from home to participate in our 40th Annual Winter Flight races. While in N.C., Michael also drove to Raleigh to participate in the Krispy Kreme Challenge 5K while consuming a dozen donuts midway.

Michael bought our ice cream with still no pineapple available. We talked about the ride so far, what he does in Bemidj, the issues he finds with running in the wintertime and much more. Just before I left home, we had our Dragon Boat races at home and Bemidji had theirs on that coming weekend. In Bemidji, they make a big deal out of watching practices and eating from food trucks on site.

On my previous trip to Bemidji after visiting Lake Itasca, I took photos of the huge Paul Bunyan and the Blue Ox statues. Michael and I snapped new photos that afternoon and I rode back to the Super Eight to complete 52 miles for the day. It was a good visit and I planned to stay in touch with Michael for the rest of the trip.

Upcoming the next day was a direct ride back to Grand Rapids on U.S. 2, some of which I had done before. I had a room that I suspected would be more my style. There wasn't much uncertainty for tomorrow and I hoped it would stay that way. Directly ahead would be Duluth and my ride along the North Shore of Lake Superior.

It was easy to sleep that night and I tried to limit any concerns for at least a day. I had ridden already along U.S. 2 for most of the distance between Bemidji and Grand Rapids. I knew the road was unusually flat and with a good bike shoulder. I didn't know much about Lake Superior and wasn't going to worry about it this day. Just ride, and have fun, was the plan. I knew there were stores along the way too, but most of them were early and late. A big section of 45 miles with little scenery made up the middle of the ride.

There was a highlight at 11 a.m. ahead, a Zoom call that I had to make with one of my employers. I work part-time for Mission Senior Living as a wellness contractor to the leadership staff. The meeting would be right when I was likely to go through the worst cellphone reception of the day. There was some traffic on the highway, and trucks in that environment can get loud. I was making good time, and I hoped to find the right spot for good reception just a few minutes before the start of the meeting. I passed a

RIVER RIDE

couple of side roads, but the overhead sun was bright and hot. I looked for some shade too.

Just three minutes before I had to make the Zoom connection, I spotted the Big Fish and the restaurant that it promotes. Someone was mowing the yard, and I saw one of the likely owners coming out of a shed. A short bike ride to that shed was perfect for preparing to ask if I could use the Big Fish for shade during my part of the call. She readily agreed and smiled quickly, pretty sure that I would have some fun talking about the huge fish with a big mouth and sharp wooden teeth about to devour my bike.

Those on the call loved the concept as I walked around the fish and showed them a wide-angle shot of it. I was allowed to make my presentation first, tell a little about this adventure and where I was going next. Just 20 minutes later, I was back on the road. A minor headwind was building, but the weather otherwise was good. I had a small bag of things ready to mail home to open more space and slightly lighten the load. My goal was to find an open post office but was not able to do it. Few of the post offices were full-day locations, so I decided to try in Duluth or on the way north from there.

My last two Mississippi River sightings happened in the early afternoon. I reminisced about how much more I knew about the great river now and remain enamored with it. I stopped for cookies a few times at White Oak and Deep River, before riding on to Grand Rapids to find my motel.

The headwind kept blowing, but a mostly flat road helped as I finished for the day at the Forest Lake Motel. I noticed this motel as I rode west just a couple days ago, an older place but neat and clean. Listening on the radio, I heard that Friday and Saturday would be really busy in town with Tall Timber Days, so I called and got the last available room. It had two beds and looked out on Forest Lake. The desk clerk was the same one that I booked the room with, and she remembered me. The clerk told me that two restaurants were next to the motel and that she thought one served breakfast all day. Another was a VFW hamburger place. Neither had what I wanted, the all-day breakfast or a veggie burger. A quick ride to the Holiday convenience store netted another F'real milkshake and plenty more.

Back in the room, I did a Facetime call with my daughter and granddaughter and showed them the lake and motel. Afterwards, I ate everything in sight and watched the wind blow, hoping it would die down by morning. I made calls to a few motels in Duluth, finally settling on one that I thought would place me about where I should be for the ride along the north shore. I knew I was paying too much but couldn't find any better option.

I was going east again on U.S. 2, all the way to Duluth. I hoped I would get another moderate ride, but Michael Zachow told me that this portion had some hills, so I was ready for anything. It was exciting to head for Duluth again, ready to go north this time. On my Northern Tier ride, I also took U.S. 2 to Duluth and remembered the struggle to get over some bridges going east. I wouldn't see those same bridges on this trip but knew nothing about the northern part of Duluth. I would handle whatever happened.

Forest Lake Motel struck me as a similar motel to those I found along Route 66. Those were old, comfortable and friendly, often with something extra. This time the extra was the big lake outside the window. I pedaled away from Grand Rapids at sunrise and was stung bigtime by a giant fly, with the burning starting at my knee and going to my feet. It was a serious sting without being officially out of town. Nothing like this had happened before that I could remember.

Riding seemed slightly uphill as I passed through Blackberry and Warba, with not much to see. Boring sameness with the landscape set in. Fleetwood was the first little town with stores, very busy with a farmer's market just shutting down as I saw vendors pull up signs and end the market. Fleetwood had the Catfish Days festival coming up. I needed a cold drink to ride in my handlebar bag. Diet Mountain Dew and some cookies were all I needed.

Next was the Fond Du Lac Indian Reservation, especially hilly. I noticed a van with bikes on the back, stopped and pointed toward me. A woman held out a canned drink and the occupants waited for me to stop. I did and enjoyed the talk with Anita and Mark Goellner. They offered me a place to stay in Duluth, but I told them that I had a room reserved and it was probably too late to cancel. At that point, I didn't know that Mark would be a major player in the last part of my trip. We had a nice conversation, but I still had additional riding to make Duluth and I expected more hills and at least moderate traffic.

The Allyndale Motel, the most expensive of the trip, had poor WiFi but a nice staff. The motel was built in 1952 and everything else worked on their historic property. It was situated so that I could get a mostly flat ride through town the next morning toward U.S. 61 and the north shore. Both Verizon and AT&T had poor service, but I got enough Wi-Fi to connect if I stood next to the office. That brings back many memories of traveling out west where often the only WiFi was in or near the office. Duluth is extremely hilly, and that remains my strongest memory from my previous visit. I arrived from the west, just as I did this time, and my first sighting of the water was from the top of a long hill that led to the downtown. My brakes worked extra hard to hold the bike back as I coasted to water level.

Still, I was excited to start toward the north shore, especially after the desk clerk told me to use Grand Avenue and Superior Street for a flat and straight shot through town. She said I would ride through the old town and eventually find London Road, the gateway to join U.S. 61. The Lake George Motel owner told me to expect hilly riding on the North Shore, and others said that U.S. 61 wasn't so bad. I would find out when I got there.

RIVER RIDE

My plan was to ride north along Lake Superior on Sunday to Silver Bay in what seemed like a short day. Few towns were ahead, but there were enough to fill my needs. I liked the old style and very quiet Allyndale Motel and slept very well, especially since the evening was already chilly before dark. I had 80 miles for the day.

Out of the motel on a cloudy morning with rain in the forecast, I rode northeast to London Road, then got my first two Taco John's breakfast burritos. Eggs, cheese and potatoes were the only ingredients I needed. I was the only customer and stopped to enjoy one of the burritos while contemplating the day. I was about to turn north to more places where I had never been, cutting my list of remaining lifetime goals.

The first views of Lake Superior came mixed with spectacular older homes on the water. I stopped at a small visitor center and found it wasn't yet open, but only for two minutes. A woman stopped, opened the doors and put her "Open" sign out before returning to me. I told her my ideas and she shared information but didn't want her picture taken. I stopped on the other side of her building and ate a burrito while skimming through the folders and flyers. The attendant told me to take a walking and bike trail all along the water as I continued north. I took the trail for a few minutes, disappointed that it was hilly, narrow and with too many turns while not continuous.

I got back on the road, usually with a decent shoulder,

and began seeing signs from the Grandma's Marathon held in June. A 5K, 10K, half-marathon and full marathon are all held at the same time on U.S. 61. Many years ago, I considered taking a big trip to run a June marathon, well past the time that a good one can be held in most of North Carolina. I never went, but now I am envisioning running the course with all the water views.

About this time, I was daydreaming as I often do and was surprised that a woman suddenly was beside me. She wasn't on a heavy bike nor was her load as big as mine, but clearly this woman was quicker than I was. Mary Beth Lawson would ride beside me and talk, then jump ahead or fall back until traffic cleared, and we continued to have a pleasant conversation while we rode. Mary was on an electric bike, and she told me so, explaining her ability to easily jump ahead. Mary's sister was meeting her at a small pull-off ahead and I stopped when she did. We talked a little more in the lot, as Mary and her sister made some suggestions of what I should see and do. Mary suggested places to have a nice meal, which I appreciated but wouldn't likely take time to do.

The only real town north of Duluth that Sunday morning was Two Harbors. Plenty of stores and traffic kept me sharp as I pedaled through the first part of town. I remembered the Two Harbors Lighthouse, first operated in 1892, and knew that I needed to head toward the water. I saw an active train station with a passenger train arriving. A couple

RIVER RIDE

was walking toward me, and I asked where the lighthouse was. She brightly said, "Oh, yes, we just left." She pointed toward the distant parking lot, and I was soon there.

I quickly toured the site, and made some pictures, one of them of an iron ore carrier that had just taken on a load right in front of me. After quickly touring the grounds of the lighthouse, I jumped back on the bike and found the best way out of town on a climb away from the water over rough roads.

Two Harbors is by far the largest town on the North Shore, but still its small with a population of less than 4,000. I made a snack and drink stop, before continuing on. Mary had told me about two tunnels coming up soon and was clear that she didn't like them. She mentioned ways to get around them, concerning me a little because some tunnels I have been in on the bike have been dark and very tight. Often, they are loud and windy inside.

I decided to ride a scenic up-and-down road beside the first tunnel's mountain after meeting three students from Middlebury College in Vermont. All of us climbed the steep scenic route and then I saw them turning around and coming back. The boys were all stopping to try their hand at rock climbing. I rode on, and soon came to the second tunnel quite ready to try it. The tunnel was well-lit, with plenty of room for my bike on the shoulder and I was very happy with the direct route.

Next was Beaver Bay, a small town and only three miles

from my stop for the night at Silver Bay. In hindsight, I should have stopped at the nice Holiday store in Beaver Bay for end-of-day food. I knew that Silver Bay was just ahead and bigger, so I pedaled on.

I had booked the Mariner Inn in Silver Bay with a phone call the night before. The rate was good, the owner was nice on the phone, and I wasn't concerned. What I found was a throwback motel of sorts. I stopped at the desk, and the clerk was pleasant and told me about the town. He said, "It's a steep climb to the town which is actually at the top of the hill. But you better hurry, because the grocery store is already closed, the pizza place will close soon, and it won't be long until the convenience store closes. Also, the climb is one mile straight up this hill behind me."

After pushing the bike to the room, I realized that most of the motel rooms must have been full, with plenty of cars in the lot. On a nice evening, I saw quite a few people sitting outside their rooms and was able to talk to two groups. I looked at the room, thought it unremarkable at a very quick glance, then unloaded some things so I could get to the convenience store on a quicker climb.

At the very top, the town was only six tenths of a mile from the motel, but I didn't tell the clerk any different. It was steep. In the convenience store, only the owner and his wife were there, and they appeared to be having a disagreement. I got $20 of stuff for the evening and part of tomorrow. Options were limited, but I did get some ice cream, a sandwich, cookies and other snacks plus a couple of drinks. I am always happy to find lemonade. In a very quick coast, I was back in front of my room, stopped to talk to the folks again on both sides of me and then entered to eat and write.

I looked around more, found very good everything including WiFi, all clean and with plenty of room. No air conditioning but a big fan was all good for me. Before I knew it, the room was getting cool, and I actually closed most of the open windows. Other over-night guests sat outside and talked, then headed inside when dark came. I met only nice people.

Unconcerned about the next day, I already had what I thought was a decent cabin in Grand Marais, the next town. I found the shower strong, hot and refreshing, and the bed very comfortable. I had all I wanted that evening after 61 miles for the day. I called back the next day and booked another night at the Mariner Inn just ahead for my return trip.

That return trip was starting to come together. I had talked with several local residents and decided not to go to Thunder Bay in Canada. Those local residents had all agreed that the drawbacks were riding two days past the Canadian border with limited supply points and not much to see in Thunder Bay. I likely would turn around near Grand Portage and then return back down the North Shore, then on to Minneapolis.

The next segment, headed north right out of Silver Bay,

began the most challenging part of the north shore ride. The desk clerk had told me not to expect many supply points, even though a few towns were listed. The first sign was for Little Marais and the next was for Taconite Harbor, pointed toward Lake Superior. Next was Schroeder with a bakery, part-time post office and an e-bike rental place. Some regular bikes were used too, but most of the riders on the e-bikes looked to be trying out something new. I did stop at the Schroeder bakery for a cinnamon scone and a cheese Danish, relaxing on the front bench for a few minutes to eat. During those few minutes, I noticed a tailwind had arrived and the serious climbing had quieted significantly. Water views had also reappeared, all three things making the ride more fun.

Next was Tofte, with a convenience store. I realized that more supply points existed than I had expected. One of the best small towns was Lutsen, pronounced Lootsin. Just a very good small general store, a post office and another store or two made up the town. I still had the bag that I wanted to send home, and this post office was open all morning. The mail carrier was coming out as I went in, a pleasant lady who stopped just as we both saw a military jet making a hard right hand turn while the jet engine screamed. The postmaster came out and watched too.

I still wanted to ship my bag of extra things acquired so far home. I asked Postmaster Laurie if I could send one of those boxes for a certain price home. She gave me the correct box, some tape and I put the bag of things in it. Meanwhile we talked about my trip and a few other things. Laurie was fun and very upbeat and engaging.

The next town was Grand Marais, the busiest tourist spot I would see on the north shore ride. Much different from any other town in the area, it had lots of restaurants, breweries, and trendy shops scattered through town. Pricing seemed highest here and I heard on the radio that available housing was hard to come by. I had what I thought was a small cabin reserved, but it turned out to be what they called a motel room. The rooms still looked like cabins; all wood paneled inside. Another place with no AC, but a good fan meant to run all day. Windows stayed open unless I closed them. At Trailside Cabins, my room was again wonderful but at least half a mile from the first part of town and more from the busier spots. And I had an unusual issue that needed to be addressed very soon. Where would I stay the next night? Available rooms were scarce.

The next morning, I would head north to Grand Portage, a town named for its importance in fur trading history. I planned to ride half a day, visit what Grand Portage had to offer and then ride back to Grand Marais for another night. Trailside had no vacancies, the nearest motel called Lund's cost nearly twice as much and others close to the water were high too. The owner at Lund's tried to help me and called a former Super Eight now named the Aspen Inn. Mr. Lund said that the place wasn't as nice as it used to be, and I knew that it was even farther from town. Instead of exploring the town, I had to weigh this situation before I could latch onto an available and affordable room.

I left Lund's and called the Aspen Inn. Their cost in a high-priced town was $100 a night, cheaper than anything I could get so far. I went by and booked it, sight unseen. Seemed a high price for a room that could have issues, but as I have often said, "I am only going to sleep there for few hours." This time, I had no real expectations.

Now with a room booked for both nights, I wanted to see the town and work through a couple of other challenges. I walked down to the town, looked at the harbor and sailboats, and stopped by Dairy Queen in hopes of a pineapple milkshake. No pineapple, yet I was shocked at the milkshake price. I still got a medium banana shake thanks to the Y Service Club. Another stop at the Holiday netted more things for the evening. I would then stop in first thing tomorrow for more as I rode north.

I made my way back to my motel/cabin and completed my writing and most of my food. Trailside didn't have ice, and the office was closed most of the time. I brought ice from the Holiday and was set for the evening, so I took time to see about another goal. It seemed on this trip that when things didn't go quite right, other related things joined them. More than going to Canada, I wanted to ride the ferry over to Isle Royale National Park. It's the least-visited National Park in the nation, only accessible by plane and boat. More of a hikers and camper's park, average attendance is 25,000 a year, which is about the same that Yellowstone gets in a day. I called several times before getting an answer and was told that the boats don't run on Tuesdays and the other days were sold out this week. She told me that I could take a chance and be waiting on site when they load the boat each morning, in hopes of getting on in place of any no shows.

What complicates all this for a cyclist and especially one who needs WiFi, was that I needed a motel room. The only ones in Grand Portage or anywhere near belonged to a casino. Those rooms were also sold out for the week. I put my name on the waiting list and actually checked back again to see if anything had changed. Laurie at Lutsen told me that her family got on the boat by waiting at the dock to see if any slots opened up. Laurie also told me that a big reenactment called the Rendezvous was scheduled for the upcoming weekend at Grand Portage. The ceremony commemorates the fur trading empire that boomed in the late 1700s and early 1800s. Multiple buildings have been reconstructed inside a stockade wall, all as a great monument to the fur traders who flourished on Lake Superior.

As dark settled in, I got inside the smallest shower of the trip so far and enjoyed it. Then it was bed, with a big picture window perfect for watching walkers and cars passing by. I watched for less than a minute. As the trip was winding down with no big issues, my sleep was again good almost every night. Tomorrow had the potential to be a fun day.

chapter 11

On to Grand Portage, then back to Minneapolis

My day ahead was simple, just riding to Grand Portage and then a return to Grand Marais after touring all there was to see. From the time I had first mentioned riding the north shore of Lake Superior, knowledgeable people had said, "Don't miss Grand Portage!" I had never been excited about furs and fur trading but knew some of the history now of that area. Now I had one last big new goal and a good plan to do it.

Rain was predicted for the evening, but I hoped to be back to Grand Marais before then. I had only one town to pass through, or so I thought. Hovland showed up as a town, but actually was only a few houses and a bakery/ABC store combined. I began to wonder if Grand Portage was a town, or at least had a store. I would need something cold to drink and some snacks for the ride back.

Thinking I was clear on the route, I was pretty sure that I only had to follow U.S. 61. When I checked with Siri, she wanted me to turn around and access another road. I hadn't seen any other real highways. But cell coverage was poor and possibly that was the reason for her error. I saw several signs calling U.S. 61 Lake Superior's North Shore Scenic Drive.

One of the most pleasurable things to do on long stretches of cycling with little to see is listening to the local radio stations. Getting a flavor of the area was always fun, and this habit seriously started with my run/walk across N.C. while chasing a baby jogger. No stations were available as I neared Grand Portage and the Canadian border. Approaching Grand Portage, I noticed a lot of signs for the casino and for the border ahead, and warnings that construction would cause serious delays that day.

My first sighting of the exit was dwarfed by a huge store and gas station. Other signs pointed to the casino and hotel, while two pointed toward Grand Portage, both on the National Park Service logo. I pedaled past the other things and coasted into a parking lot for the visitor center. Oddly, at a time when I thought the traffic was light, the parking lot was quite full of vehicles and people.

I leaned my bike against a good wall and went inside, thinking only for a few seconds about the possibility someone would take the bike and my gear. I took my wallet, iPad and phone inside, but the rest of my adventure sat on those two wheels. I knew it would be there when I got back after hundreds of similar occurrences.

The visitor center was large and situated on several levels. I had a feeling that maybe some of the staff might have overnight space there, since few homes and only the casino motel were close by. The displays were wonderful, especially lifelike figures who were dressed in period costumes and carrying huge amounts of fur weight on their backs. The French and local Native Americans were highlighted as well. A short video explaining the fur trade at Grand Portage was interesting.

I began to wonder where the reconstructed buildings and the monument were. The park ranger at the desk told me to just follow the sidewalk down toward the water. As I entered the area, I was amazed to find a huge stockade built and preserved to show how life would have been in the late 1700s. Many of the prominent buildings had been reconstructed, furnished and manned with volunteers who demonstrated methods and customs of that time. Striking to me were the many Indian teepees set up for habitation in winters of extreme cold. I simply couldn't imagine winter nights that sometimes dipped into the minus 30's would be survivable with just coverings of birchbark. Summer gardens were growing vegetables that day, a perfect day in the upper 60s. Outdoor ovens were ready to make bread and the bigger buildings were set up for grand meetings and parties. At any given time, as many as 1,000 people had lived or visited inside the stockade. The statement that keeps coming back is that this area has winter for seven months a year, and the rest is summer.

I toured some of the buildings and listened in on the explanatory talks addressing what they were used for. I asked one of the hosts where the actual monument to the fur traders is, and he said, "We get that a lot. All of this, the buildings, the dock and the stockade are all one big monument to those men and women who lived here and carried on the fur trade."

With that said, this monument was phenomenal! I could have stayed for hours looking around, talking with people and taking photos. I had a long ride back to Grand Marais, and the raindrops were already starting to fall. I walked back to the parking lot where I left the bike. Of course, it was still there, and the lot was still very busy.

Bill Kuhn and wife Marianne walked to the bike and asked me, "Where are you going?" I told him about the current journey and about some of the others in the past. We talked for a few minutes as the rain got harder, then exchanged cards and headed away from the National Park. I never had to use my National Park Service Senior Pass, bought six years ago for $10 and always good for free entry. At Grand Portage, there was no cost for anyone. Grand Portage was one of the highlights of my trip.

Entering Canada near Grand Portage would have to wait on another visit. Construction was delaying traffic, the border was at least 6 ½ miles each way and no telling how long entry across the border would take each time. I stopped at the huge convenience store, truck stop and post office for a cold drink and some snacks for the return trip. So far from other towns, prices were very reasonable, and supplies were plentiful. I suspect that this building was the center of activity in the area.

I began the ride back toward Grand Marais and almost immediately waved to the Kuhns as they passed back by. They were camping in Grand Marais. That short conversation with Bill was about to become very significant. Leaving Grand Portage would now point me south and west for the first time.

Rain came and went as I rode south, most of it steady or light and not uncomfortable in temperatures just below 70 degrees. Traffic wasn't heavy either, and I already knew the road was good. Arriving back in Grand Marais, I stopped for evening food at the Holiday again, then began the ride through town and up the long hill toward the west. Just as I began the hill, a motorist yelled, "Hey, you dropped your rain jacket back at the last intersection!" I rode back and found the jacket undamaged and mostly clean. After securing it to the bike, I rode up the long hill to the Aspen Inn and checked into the room.

I found a clean and wonderful room for me, with nothing important lacking. No AC again, but I didn't need it. There was a huge heater in the room, which I am sure gets lots more activity than any cooling unit would. I was in a one-level segment, with open windows, and a huge room and bathroom. My bike and I both had a wonderful evening and night inside, while a thunderstorm came and went outside. Although there were other patrons, I didn't hear anyone during the night. After 73 miles for the day, this was the perfect location.

I've been asked often what I do at night, especially after my writing is done. I start with the writing and eating as soon as I settle in. Then I answer any messages sent during the day. I check the news on my iPad mini. In 21 nights on the road for Part II, I don't think I turned on the TV more than 3-4 times, once for a ballgame and several times for weather. On a typical evening, after all is done with messages, I enjoy a hot shower, one that loosens all the muscles before heading for bed about 10 p.m. Some nights were later, as you'll see shortly, but only a few. Once in bed, I seldom had any trouble sleeping unless I had a specific reason for rising even earlier. If a problem situation was expected, I may get up a few minutes early to address it. Otherwise, I was up about an hour before heading out. Packing and distributing the gear, a very light breakfast, the news and a few more messages usually would have me ready to hit the door with enough daylight to be seen. Late summer riding means that the days are shorter by a minute or so each morning. I wanted the bike and my flashing red light to be easily visible.

My job on this day was a challenging one. I was set to return to Silver Bay and another evening at the Mariner Motel. On the way, I wanted to see several things I had bypassed on the ride north. And I hoped to hear on the radio how much rain had fallen and whether it was widespread. There was a great community radio station in this area called WTIP that covered all things North Shore and had wonderful music too. I have a new appreciation for North Shore folk music and have since listened to it several times from home. The last 20 miles would be the most challenging hills of the remaining cycling before St. Paul-Minneapolis. I dreaded a section of the poor road shoulder that put me very close to likely the worst traffic of the day.

The weather was wonderful first thing, traffic moderate and I knew that the first stop was Lutsen, where I had met Postmaster Laurie two days before. As I rode into the parking lot of the post office and country store, I saw Laurie running out the front door, waving. She told me she lives in Grand Marais and had already seen me riding toward Lutsen that morning. Laurie set up her workstation at the front door to not miss me. What a huge lift that was!

Laurie told me more about some of her travel, and I told her that I couldn't work out getting on the sightseeing boat at Grand Portage. This time! I still had on my long-sleeve shirt, but Laurie told me she considered the morning's weather hot. I was glad for a few more degrees. I waved goodbye and promised to send her one of these books, and some more too. I grabbed an egg-and-cheese bagel at the country store and continued south.

Tofte was next, with a Holiday convenience store that carried the World's Best Donuts. I had promised the young cyclists from Middlebury College that I would try them.

Prior to today, I had not been in Grand Marais when the main WBD store was open, but several of the Holiday stores advertised them. I got a Long John, with maple topping and immediately ate it. It was very good, but I would need at least one more to consider whether it was the best in the world!

A life-sized Sasquatch was holding my bike when I came out of the store. I was able to take it back. On to Schroeder again. Just three miles after the long-john, I had a refill on the cheese Danish and the cinnamon scone. My legs would be powered by pastries all the way to Silver Bay.

Next, I passed through the area with all the E-bikes riding around. I saw one interesting group with a mom, dad, a couple of kids and grandparents. On through the challenging hills, a building headwind and the bad shoulders, I finally spotted the turn off for Silver Bay and the Mariner. That ride of 56 hard fought miles felt way tougher than it should have.

Several good things happened at the Mariner. I told the desk guy that I was trying to figure out my route from Duluth to the Twin Cities and he suggested researching the Munger Trail. I had not heard of it, but his suggestion started discussions that eventually put me on that trail. I rode to the top of the Silver Bay hill and grabbed food again, this time starting at a small grocery store. The Mariner room is just perfect for me and won a top three on the best showers of the trip. On the radio that day, I learned that the rain had dumped close to an inch on some areas, more than they had seen since July Fourth. Much more was needed, but this particular drought had caused Lake Superior to drop a half inch in water volume, during a time when it would usually gain two inches. These are significant when you figure that Lake Superior holds 10% of the world's fresh water.

After yet another perfect night at the Mariner, I pedaled away knowing that this would be my last full day along Lake Superior. And it would be a busy day. The wind was gusting early at Silver Bay but was a side wind to start. Yesterday's headwind was the toughest of the trip, and I hoped to get a reprieve today.

Just south of Silver Bay, I had to ride a very tight strip of narrow shoulder that was mostly filled with rumble strips. Since I was early, the traffic was not yet heavy enough to matter. I had an early goal to visit the Split Rock Lighthouse, built in 1910 and one of the most photographed attractions in Minnesota. It sits on the top and edge of a sheer 133-foot cliff and was built because of the many shipwrecks in the area.

I rode into the park about 8 a.m. and found the visitor center and, you guessed it, it was closed. A staff member was walking in and told me that the center would open at 10 a.m.. She did tell me that I could see the lighthouse by following the trail to the water's edge and looking up. It was the only option since I couldn't wait until 10 a.m. I grabbed my iPad, walked down the trail and saw several others doing the same. I was shocked that summer hours were shorter than winter hours. The staff person told me, "Well, we can't be open all the time!"

I made a few photos from the rocks below and met Julie and her dog, Tucker. They were traveling by car and had friends at Gooseberry Falls campground, where we both would be going next. Julie climbed a long set of steps and got better photos of the lighthouse because she was able to shade out the bright morning sun. I did the same and was much happier with my photos as well.

Next came a short ride to Gooseberry Falls State Park, the second attraction of the day. I saw Julie and Tucker right away, among what looked like a packed house. The parking lot was more than full. Julie told me that the Middle Falls were the best and I totally agreed. Quite a few adults and even more teens were in the water, which had to be very cold.

I knew that Two Harbors was the next town ahead. Just on the north side of it, I also knew that the third attraction of the day was close by. I had seen Betty's Pies on the trip north but wanted to save it until the return trip. I saw major construction on U.S. 61 in front of Betty's parking lot but didn't have any trouble getting in. I estimated 50 cars in the late morning parking lot.

Not sure what or how I could order, I saw people going inside, people eating at picnic tables and waiting at a take-out spot. I parked the bike and walked to the take-out spot, amazingly at the best possible time because no one was in line. I asked about what was available and was shown a chart of the flavors. I ordered a slice of Bombleberry, a mixture of several berries, and a slice of Maple Pecan. About five minutes later, I got the pie slices and ate the Maple Pecan one right away. The Bombleberry rode along until I got hungry about 10 miles later, and undoubtedly it was the best pie I had ever eaten.

Exiting to go south was hard with the construction and limited space for a bike. I walked the bike probably 1,000 feet, then had enough shoulder again to ride. The headwind was again building and was especially strong when I re-entered Two Harbors. It pushed me back hard and I was glad to leave town.

My destination for the evening was Mark and Anita Goellnor's house on the northern side of Duluth. Mark and Anita are the couple who stopped in their van and waited on me with a cold drink the previous weekend. We stayed in touch, and they invited me to their house with the promise of advice to get through Duluth on the best track to Minneapolis. Mark gave me directions to their house that involved at least one terrific climb as, in Mark's words, "We are significantly higher than Lake Superior."

Upon arrival, I found this beautiful house on 20 acres of wooded land and two wonderful people genuinely interested in my ride, partly because Mark is an endurance cyclist as well. We had a wonderful dinner, complete with chocolate ice cream topped with raspberries. No charge to the service club on this one.

Mark helped me with a plan to ride from Duluth to Hinkley, Minnesota, about halfway to the Twin Cities. Heavy rain was predicted overnight, but with lessening showers after daylight. I hoped to follow Mark's directions through downtown Duluth, then link to the Willard Munger Trail on to Hinckley. The Munger Trail is a rail trail, also the same one mentioned by the desk clerk at the Mariner Inn in Silver Bay. My goal was 92 miles for the day. All looked great until I made my first call to find a room in Hinckley. None were available, and I called all the options listed. I gave up way too late and went to bed. The accommodations issue had raised a serious concern. As one of my favorite sayings goes, "Nothing left to do but do it!"

I would work on the problem as I rode away. I was confident. And during this evening, I learned that Lake Superior is about the same size as South Carolina, about 31,700 square miles.

The next two days were going to be exciting. Mark had told me a few days before that I would have about seven miles into Duluth and all of it would be downhill. That is how much climbing was done from Lake Superior to the Goellnor's house. I was only a little worried about all the challenges of the morning — the rain, the low visibility, pedaling into a busy town, seemingly no availability for a room at my goal distance.

RIVER RIDE

As my good friend and former Salisbury Post nighttime editor Paris Goodnight would say, "So tell me about the good things!" I was already doing an inventory. The wind was behind my bike, traffic seemed light, and I had good riding lanes even when I entered town. I didn't struggle much following directions, even though I had to take a detour. People gave me room, and 18 miles flew by. I had a decision to make, so I stopped quickly as the only customer at yet another Taco John's. Eggs, potatoes and cheese on two burritos. Mark was back at home trying to help me find a room, plus he confirmed with a friend that I could use his camping trailer in Barnum, still well short of where I wanted to end this day.

Just before bed, I made calls to eight places, of which two were no longer open, the rest were full and two were ridiculously gouging people. The casino hotel offered a room at over $400 but alerted me that I could get a free spa treatment with the room. I would have never forgiven myself for taking that room. Two motels blamed a two-night weekend country concert series, but a chain motel with a posted rate of $79 had suddenly doubled it.

At almost a direct shot to Hinckley from Duluth, I got on the Munger Trail and watched some other possible routes fade away behind the trees. One cyclist told me to take U.S. 23, but I was committed to following Mark's suggestion. The trail seemed all uphill for several miles and the rain continued. I saw few people but did ask a couple of rollerbladers what they thought of the route. They knew little and were just enjoying a short ride in the rain. I decided to keep rolling, thinking that the terrain would eventually get better. Railroad construction engineers were phenomenal at finding the best routes. One of my mantras on the bike remains, "If your route parallels a railroad track, then you are on the flattest route possible." This has played out time and again over the years. If the tracks leave, then beware!

No towns presented themselves early on the trail, but eventually the terrain flattened out and a few towns were posted ahead. I rode through Mahtowa and Carlton, then passed through an especially scenic portion of the trail. U.S. 61 ran parallel most of the time at this point. I stopped for a few photos and noticed a large family walking ahead. We all started talking, especially the dad, Kevin, and I. He is a bike racer and I just felt connected to his family. Kevin asked if I needed anything, and I thought of my phone with a lower charge than I would need for a possibly long day.

After such a fast start, the pace had been dragging once I got on the trail. Recently I had been able to pick up the pace, but still had no idea where I would spend the night. Kevin and family walked on to a nearby park, and I met them at their van. I gave these total strangers my phone to charge while I continued to ride. We all laughed about that. Kevin told me where to meet them, a store that sounded like the best one around. Finally making good time, I thought after they left that I should have just given them one of my bags so I could slack pack a little, the term used by hikers when someone else carries their pack.

Things were looking up, with the weather improving, and Barnum was not far ahead if I chose to use Mark's friend's camper. Unsure of the food and WiFi situation, I wanted to keep my eyes open for a farther solution. I was considering camping beside the road, and Kevin gave me a couple ideas.

After about 90 minutes, I found Kevin's family at TJ's, one of those country stores that has everything, including a playground for the kids. All the family was relaxing on the playground. I had decided to just keep riding, making a long day out of it even if I couldn't find a place to overnight with WiFi. It seemed that no campgrounds were close.

We talked about the drought, Kevin's racing, what I did back home and much more. We would have become great friends had we lived close together. Kevin noticed that his cellphone radar showed an intense storm approaching the area. The family suggested that I grab some food at TJ's. While inside, the owner suggested I set up my tent in a shelter she had out back, but I thanked her and said, "I just want to make more miles today. If I don't, tomorrow will be impossible. I have to pick up a car on Sunday morning at the Twin Cities airport."

As we parted company, the kids all waved, One of them, little Nicholas, ran over and said, "We are going to look you up and follow the rest of your ride!" I was excited to hear this. He had said nothing to me before that. Another nice memory of great people.

I rode on through another pretty part of the Munger Trail. On the radio, weather reports made the storm look serious. I got a text from Mark in Duluth about the bad weather reports. Lightning was in the area. Quickly, the rain started to spatter, and I took a big leap and called the Barnum Inn in Barnum. I told the owner that I was on a bike and asked if she had a single room. In rapid succession, she said, "I am sorry but I don't, where are you now?" Over the years, I have learned to have some optimism when I get a serious answer quickly followed by a question. Without missing a beat, she said, "I have a room, but we haven't planned to start renting it yet. We are doing some work on it."

Not even knowing what the cost was, I jumped ahead of my normal process and said, "If you can get the room ready, I will take it." She told me to ride that way and she would have the room ready. Even though I would be caught way short of the miles needed, I would get out of this storm and hopefully have a restful evening. On the radio, reports of severe hail and wind damage began to come in. I just kept pedaling through steady rain, lightning and thunder. With almost every pedal stroke, I pushed hard as possible, glad that the rain was falling in an area that needed it but ready to get out of this particular storm.

I went to sleep knowing what lay ahead, by far the biggest challenge of any day in Part I or II of this book and one of my biggest of all time on the bike. The perfect day had to

RIVER RIDE

begin the next morning!

chapter 12

*Barnum on to the Twin Cities;
as close to a perfect day as possible*

By stopping in Barnum yesterday afternoon during the rainstorm, I raised the challenge to the maximum level for today. Instead of finding a way to balance the mileage between Friday and Saturday, I pushed today's needed mileage to around 110. The rental car would be waiting at the airport on Sunday morning. All I had to do was get close enough to access the airport early. Sounds easy, doesn't it?

The severe weather didn't hit Barnum yesterday, but it did hit other areas hard. Large hail hit Minneapolis and talk of nearby power outages on the radio took prominence. We did have another round of rain last night at my motel, but nothing concerning.

I planned my route, stocked up on some supplies, told a few people about my goal and went to bed the earliest that I had during the whole adventure. I wanted the earliest possible start, so I was out the door with only marginal light. The man in the next motel room was outside and began to ask about the whole adventure. Already a little on edge with the time and challenges ahead, I took a few minutes to describe where I had been and was hopefully going today.

Then I wished him well and he did the same for me.

Then I pedaled out to the street and retraced my route back to the Munger Trail, all downhill this time. I passed a local school and noticed that something was happening. Cars were coming in, and lots of people were already moving at just after 6 a.m. I thought about the possibility of a running race at the school as I waved to a couple of the parking attendants.

Just as I reached the trail, I met a very fast female runner, then a couple guys behind her, and noticed they were wearing lights and reflective wear. Those three and then some more runners in the distance were running toward me on the trail. As I pedaled by each runner, we greeted each other, a nice way to start the day. I knew that I was watching a long-distance relay race happen around me with a front row seat.

For the last five years or so, I have traveled to Nevada to participate in a similar event called the Reno-Tahoe Odyssey, a 178-mile team run around part of Lake Tahoe. In our case, a team of 12 runners used two vans to alternately take turns running segments around the clock. I didn't know the details here but vowed to find out more. Knowing that I couldn't lose focus during the day, meeting these runners lost in their own competition would boost my efforts too.

I saw signs later and looked up the Ragnar Relay. Water stops and checkpoints were placed along the paved Munger Trail. Nothing passed the time better for me and I was never delayed. Hundreds of runners were doing my route in reverse from St. Paul to Duluth, about 200 miles.

The first town was Moose Lake, where the Munger Trail disappears for awhile and then resumes on down the road. I saw the ending sign, saw runners coming at me, then tried to find the continuation point. I joined the wrong bike path and soon realized that I was beginning to turn east instead of south. I retraced my route briefly and saw a sign for County Road 61 and followed it. Almost immediately, the Munger Trail and the relay runners were beside me. Once I realized that there were lots more runners remaining, I rejoined the trail again using the others as part of my motivation.

Just before finding the continuation point, I came close to a serious mishap. A man had three very small dogs all of whom appeared to be on leashes. Suddenly one of them breaks loose and runs at me, somehow going under the bike without causing a crash. The man yelled, "Sorry!" as I pedaled on, thankful to still be upright.

Still cool enough to be pleasant, I saw several of the van checkpoints where runners got out and others got in the vans. Many of the vans were painted with unique team names or sayings.

I passed through Sturgeon Lake, Willow River, Rutledge and Finlayson with its unique old depot. Runners kept coming toward me. At Hinkley, or specifically just before it, I saw C.R. 61 200 yards to my left just before the end of the Munger Trail. The relay runners had passed this point too, although their water stops remained. I knew that most of my remaining riding would be on or near 61 which was fine with me. It did cross under or over Interstate 35 a couple of times, with both times leaving me with a good road to ride. Traffic remained minimal.

Remaining towns that I passed through were Pine Lake, Rock Creek, Rush City, Harris, Forest Lake, Stacy, Hugo and finally White Bear. The miles kept rolling by and I was confident that I could make the distance if the bike stayed together. My prayers were offered constantly that all would remain good. I was having the time of my life! It is for days like this that I love these adventures. I know all about the challenges and the good times. Mixing a certain set of challenges and over the top progress when needed most was impossible to beat. I was pumped, but two issues were on my mind.

Now that it looked like I might just make the 110 miles, I needed a place to stay. I texted Michael Zachow in Bemidji, asking for help in finding an affordable place to stay about 10 miles from St. Paul. If he could do it, I had a plan for tomorrow to reach the airport easily.

Over the last 10 days, I had some periodic problems with my gear shifter on the right handlebar. This shifter adjusted the series of nine gears in each of the three major rings. About 35 miles out, I couldn't make it shift. If I stopped, I could force the shifter to move, but I couldn't do it while sitting on the bike. When shifters are properly used, the hills are lessened by the right gear choice. Once the shifter locked up, it was just like riding an old style one-speed bike. I prayed that the terrain would remain reasonable, and it did. The bike is in one of my farm sheds as I write this, and the gears are still locked.

I made the front door of the Emerald Inn in White Bear, almost exactly 10 miles from the Twin Cities Airport. Michael did great work and texted me within minutes with the info while I kept pedaling. I called and got the weekday rate for a Saturday and found a nice motel with places to eat within a few blocks. My arrival was just before sunset, using just about all of the perfect day that I had hoped for all along.

For once, I need not be in a hurry. I put the bike in the room with the help of an elevator. Then walked to Wendy's and loaded up. God had once again brought me safely to the end of the ride. My Frosty that night was the best ice cream of the trip! Thank you, Y Service Club! The pressure was off and my plan to get to the airport was special too!

Bill Kuhn turned out to be an interesting guy, way beyond his own cross country bike adventure. Bill stayed in touch after we talked at Grand Portage and then he found out that my trip would end in Minneapolis-St. Paul. We made plans to have breakfast on Sunday before he dropped me and the bike off at the airport.

Bill was the last of a series of people who became a significant part of my Mississippi River/Lake Superior journey. I will revisit him and the others as I close out this cycling trip, spread over two summers. At no other time have so many quality people been involved in my travels for days past the time I met them. I hope to stay in touch with many of them.

Part II's conclusion is just ahead. New Orleans is screaming my name, even though that city concludes Part I.

conclusion

The Pursuit of the Perfect Day!
My ride along the Mississippi and North Shore
was more than that!

In July 2022, I headed north to Dubuque, Iowa, by car for an adventure that I knew would take parts of two summers. I talked with Michelle Rahe at the Dubuque, Iowa, visitor center about things to see in her area, but also what she knew about heading south along the Mississippi. I remember that she told me that cycling would be dangerous on the Great River Road with cars being so close. She was worried, but I was not.

I stopped at the Field of Dreams, my favorite destination for Part I of this adventure. Dubuque itself was a fun town too, especially since I spent two nights there. The Mississippi River Museum was the best I saw over the length of the river.

My quest began for pineapple ice cream, and finally the Y Service Club honored their lifetime pledge again. I never once found pineapple north of Dubuque the next summer.

Mark Twain's Hannibal, Missouri, was my next favorite location, a second place where I spent two nights. Vicksburg was good too but could have been better had they offered tours. The Nathez Trace Parkway was my favorite riding location, especially since so few vehicles and no trucks used it on a pouring rainy day.

Civil War history was at almost every turn south of Iowa, and I continued to stop at every historical marker. I was challenged to cross the Mississippi River at Memphis and was amazed how a pedestrian bridge could be so well done just a few feet from a train bridge.

I loved racing the huge thunderstorm in Baton Rouge and visiting the amazing World War II Museum in New Orleans, a must-see for all. I learned about the earthquake history in New Madrid, Mississippi. Nothing was better than making fast time while cycling on the Mississippi interstates, which I did often.

Roads got worse heading south, state by state. I have never seen so much trash on roads as in Mississippi and Louisiana. South of Baton Rouge, the roads were the worst I have ever seen, leaving me no options to avoid the potholes and likely flats from metal and glass. I had them too, with three on the last day. We found a small chunk of glass in the rear tire, impossible to feel with the fingers and possibly the culprit for all three flat tires.

I will likely never solve the mystery of the missing motel in Muscatine, Iowa.

Part I of the trip had three special people involved, all deserving mention. Layne Logan stopped on the street in Vicksburg with a bottle of water and eventually answered my questions for several days. Cheryl Linyear tried to keep my bike off the Amtrak train back to Salisbury and we ended up becoming friends over the whole scenario. I hope to see her again when I return to New Orleans.

David Bourg got me out of a tough situation in Louisiana. He stopped to help repair a flat, then when that tire again went flat, he drove back to pick me up late on a Saturday evening. Then he took me into New Orleans when he had other plans. His effort got me home on time, and I hope to see him again on my return to ride the last 30 miles of this journey. The discussion that evening was likely the best I have ever had associated with a bike ride. Thank you, David, for "paying it forward." We won't publish the book until those miles are done.

Many of the towns south of Iowa were failing financially, with numerous unused storefronts. People seemed less friendly and more cautious in general than I saw the next summer while cycling north.

I count myself very fortunate to make these adventure-filled bicycle trips. Lots of factors, including my health and ability to get away, add to this blessing. Recapping Part II's 19 days on the bike and three days of driving made me happier than if I won a lottery.

When I first started cycling these adventures, I told people it would be the scenery that made it wonderful. How wrong I was! Yes, the scenery was great this time and usually is. Anything to do with the Mississippi River stands out. I saw the biggest freshwater lake in the world and all kinds of interesting sights to do with both. The Grand Portage

Monument, actually a late 1700s stockade, trading post and fur storage facility with room for 1,000 people, is very hard to beat. I saw several waterfalls and lighthouses and more humorous things than I can count.

Those things are just a few memories I have brought home with me. I learned within 10 days of beginning my first cross country trip in 2013 that it is not the scenery at all that makes the trip memorable. It's of course the people, and I am going to name a few with the maybe futile hope that I won't forget someone. I started way back near Marquette and Macgregor when Jon Stravers and I met outside the town's post office. He gave me endless help on how to proceed on the upper Mississippi, and he made it fun. Then I got to use the knowledge of Michael Zachow in Bemidji, mostly on how to proceed around the upper Mississippi near Lake Itasca. He didn't stop there, because of the very last day of my ride from Barnum to the St. Paul area, I asked him for more help. I needed someone to help me find a reasonable motel just 10 miles from St. Paul and Michael did that with the Emerald Inn, an exact 10 miles away. Very special!

Then it was Dr. Mark and Anita Goellner who I met when she held a cold drink out to me from their van door on my ride toward Duluth. I ended up spending a night with them, and Mark helped me plan the route for the last part of the ride from Duluth on down to Hinckley. Andy Eller got me out of the gravel road maze that Siri put me in.

RIVER RIDE

I rode and talked with Mary Beth Lawson as she gave me tips from the seat of her electric bike. I saw Postmaster Laurie Dhein at Lutsen twice and she had tips too, but the best thing was her rushing to the post office door to make sure I was stopping on the second morning I passed by.

I met Bill Kulp at Grand Portage from where he communicated the rest of the way, then actually took me and the bike to the airport to pick up the rental car for the trip home. Allison Tuck arranged yet another fantastic journey with the one-way rental cars for this trip. Rayna Gardner managed the whole thing again and finally gave me the approval to do the trip just a few days before it started.

I got to see China Grove's Ethan Horne and his fiancée, Kim, in Minneapolis, and he rode with me for a day on the bikes. When Ethan and I unloaded our bikes and passed them through the back of a railroad tank car walkway, I thought that such a thing could only happen on a great bike adventure. We stayed in touch nearly every day, with me picking his brain for knowledge of the area. All this, and I was only riding for 19 days! And all these people helped and wanted to do more, just an incredible heartwarming package.

Near to my heart is the bottomless Y Service Club ice cream, the ever-present Kwik Trip and Holiday convenience stores, the World's Best Donuts, Betty's Pies (the Bombleberry is absolutely the best ever) and the Mariner, Lake George, and Water's Edge Motels. Among many other things, I enjoyed all the tailwinds and flat terrain I could get along all 2,552 miles of the Mississippi. History made its impact with the homes of Charles Lindbergh and Laura Ingalls Wilder. I hated the flies and mosquitoes, but they mostly left me alone, didn't care for the bluff riding, and had only the one brief encounter with Bigfoot when he wanted my bike. I did get a minor concussion and a bruised rib from a fall on the gravel road under construction. Now a month later, my head and ribs appear to have returned to normal, as has my running. Thanks, Carol O'Brien, for the honey; I have nearly finished it.

I told the real story of the crappiest motel ever, and I made more new and lasting friends over these two rides than probably any two rides ever before.

Finally, my thanks go to the sponsors who made all this happen. See the complete list in the acknowledgments. Your contributions are so valued and important! Worth one more mention are Elizabeth Cook, who continues to teach me about writing, Andy Mooney, the magician who makes these adventures look so good in the Post and the book, and then always the readers who carry me through the hard times. Lastly, thanks to God for riding with me each and every day, good or bad!

addendum

**Finally getting it done!
The Mississippi River ride is now complete**

With the rest of the book complete, I finally seized the opportunity to get the remaining miles to New Orleans under my bike wheels. The experience made for a wonderfully challenging mini-adventure.

In August of 2022, I planned the Mississippi River final day's ride from Baton Rouge, Louisiana on to New Orleans. Without any real concerns, I had heard about a chance of showers in the afternoon with some heavy thunderstorms in the area. The distance of the ride was just over 80 miles and there were no real hills. I even expected to finish with some time to walk around the city.

I started early, as usual. The roads were often in poor repair and had lots of metal in the form of screws, nails, wire and lots of glass. All are big concerns to a cyclist. The rain came early in the afternoon with big winds and heavy downpours. I waited out the worst of it in a store. Just afterwards, I had the first flat tire of the whole trip just over halfway of the day's ride to New Orleans. Then I had two more and all my tubes were used up. Darkness wasn't far away. Very fortunate to have an option, I called David Bourg, a resident of nearby Paulina who I had just met when he stopped to help on the last tube replacement. I had waited at the Marathon convenience store and was told that part of the store with tables and a place to sit would close at 9 p.m. No Uber responses came with a vehicle big enough to carry my bike.

David had to talk to his wife, Lynne, because they had something planned that included work on their pool area. Lynne wanted him to stay home to do the work since he had surgery planned for the next week. David called me back and said he was on the way. He drove me into the city, a round trip of over 80 miles for him. All he wanted was for me to pay it forward!

We had an hour to talk during the drive and we shared life experiences. I was extremely disappointed to not be able to finish the bike ride that day, especially when all looked so promising early in the day. I did not complete what finally amounted to 36 miles of the bicycle journey along the river. Out of tubes and with no reasonable alternatives, I had a train to catch to Salisbury. Finishing this portion of the whole Mississippi adventure had been on my mind for the better part of 15 months, but even more so in the last few weeks since the northern portion of the river ride was completed in August 2023.

I envisioned 3-4 days to fix this. I included cycling north of Laplace to a Marathon convenience store, exactly where David picked me up after the final flat. Then most of another day to ride on into New Orleans to Jackson Square to

RIVER RIDE

complete the southern ride with several photos to prove it. And I wanted to visit David and Lynne Bourg, especially after their invitation to stay with them. David is an engineer for Valero's refinery in Norco, very near to LaPlace.

My drive to LaPlace got off to a slow start on Friday, Oct. 20, due to wind, rain and hail in China Grove and interstate slowdowns due to several major wrecks in the area. It was the first hail I had seen while outside in several years. A tour bus had collided with several other vehicles in our area on Interstate 85. Traffic was rerouted earlier in the afternoon. When I started, the interstate was open but only making very slow progress.

I left just after 4 p.m. and only made 100 miles in the first three hours, but then the pace picked up. I slept a few hours in two different rest areas. While listening to baseball playoffs on the radio, I probably stopped a little too early. I didn't fall asleep as quickly as I hoped, then slept only fitfully. The second stop was when I really needed the rest. I was tired, my eyes were closing, and I was hoping for a rest area soon. This time, I slept well for most of three hours.

I arrived just past noon on Saturday after changing to the Central Time Zone. I quickly rode to the Marathon store, had the same grumpy cashier from a year ago, and returned to Laplace. 14 miles done and two photos taken! This part was simple, and I put it behind me quickly.

With a room at the Days Inn, I ran in the dark on Sunday morning, then hopped on the bike during one of the heaviest fogs I have ever experienced. David Bourg later told me that the extreme fog is caused by the nearby Mississippi. My red light was working, and I had plenty of shoulder to ride on. With not a real hill in sight, I rode south into the gradually lifting fog, but for the first 10 miles nothing could be seen farther than 30 yards in any direction.

Whether or not to ride on the levee into New Orleans to avoid the city was on my mind. I decided to take the city head-on, partly because riding the levee would extend the ride by five miles each way.

Following my old friend, U.S. Highway 61, I went straight into the city where 61 is also called Tulane Avenue. Traffic had remained light, and riding was easy. I made a few turns to ride through the French Quarter which was jammed with people and too many cars. I tried to follow what was supposed to be a bike lane. Cars were just parked on top of it, and nobody seemed to follow traffic lights or signs prohibiting turns. Lots of people who appeared just a tad odd were on display.

I rode right up to an extremely crowded Jackson Square, what I considered the goal for the day. The Mississippi is wide and beautiful here; the steamboats are moored nearby with street performers and vendors everywhere. Horse-drawn carriages and beignets are close also. People watching is at its best, yet nobody seems in a big hurry. I took an hour to watch the river, with a few massive ships and plenty of smaller vessels going by. I saw two steamboats depart on their tours. Most remarkable was a military jet flyover to commemorate my ride completion! I know in my heart, the completed adventure was big for them too!

The ride back over the same road was uneventful, except for the first time I saw all the massive refineries along the river without fog or darkness. One after another. I realized how massive the refineries actually are. They are even more spectacular when seen at night, with all the lights and a few fires burning from smokestacks.

I visited David and Lynne, had some wonderful ice cream and fought a few mosquitoes before leaving at almost dark. The mosquitoes were relentless, I found two the next morning in my truck and the last one the next morning. During the visit, David and I recapped our meeting the year before and how much he helped me out of a tight spot. We also talked more about our lives and families, and especially our goals ahead. They hope to vacation in North Carolina. They had completed the pool that was an issue when he left to come take me to New Orleans. They had also remodeled a beautiful kitchen.

My drive home was anything but uneventful. I suddenly lost power in my truck just north of Montgomery, Alabama. Without any warning, the truck slowed dramatically while I was in the fast lane at just under 80 mph. I simply put on the right turn signal and somehow found a way to get to the right-side shoulder. The truck would start but would not keep running. A part called a MAF sensor went bad and got me a wonderful AAA ride on Brian Martin's rollback and excellent service at Son's Ford in Auburn, Alabama. I did have to wait overnight for the part. It arrived late morning, and with the help of Veronica in customer service, I was on the road again by noon. I did get to run through Auburn University and saw the spectacular football stadium. I could only imagine a thrilling Auburn/Alabama game being played with me in the stands.

Friday night through Tuesday night, 1,551 driving miles, two time zones and 74 cycling miles were all I needed to complete the Mississippi River. I wouldn't have missed a minute of it! Thanks for riding along, once again! I hope you enjoyed this addendum. I am working on what's next.

• • •

My gear list for both Parts I and II remained virtually the same from recent trips. Overall, here are the highlights:

My 2014 Surly Long Haul Trucker bike keeps doing a great job! Our local bike shop, Skinny Wheels, repaired the shifting issue by taking it apart and doing a thorough cleaning. Eric and Scott also get huge credit for putting me on thorn-resistant tubes. I had no flats on Part II or this addendum ride to New Orleans. Never have I seen so much trash of the flat-inducing variety as I did on the roads of Louisiana. If you ride this way, I suspect the trash will still be there.

The Brooks B-17 seat is perfect for me, and although

well-worn, I would not think of changing it for another. Saddle issues are never a concern.

Two Ortlieb panniers could not be replaced with anything better in my opinion.

The matching Ortlieb handlebar bag is also perfect for my needs. I carry the things I need quickly like wallet, cellphone, iPad and now my hot weather iced drinks. Everything else goes in the panniers.

My tent did not get used on these trips nor did the sleeping bag and sleeping pad. They did ride the whole way for Part I and II but did not make the addendum ride into New Orleans. The tool kit got some minor use, as did the cycling rain jacket.

I anticipate no major changes in gear going forward.

DAVID FREEZE

The Field of Dreams movie site.

Freeze's loaded bike, ready to ride along the Mississippi River.

RIVER RIDE

First sighting of a riverboat while riding through Bettendorf, Iowa.

Huck Finn and Tom Sawyer statue in Hannibal, Missouri.

Freeze whitewashes the Tom Sawyer fence in Hannibal, Missouri.

Flood doors to shut out the river in Cape Girardeau, Missouri.

RIVER RIDE

A towboat pushes barges north on the Mississippi River.

The 1854 Courthouse in New Madrid, Mississippi, site of a major Civil War battle and where the river once ran backwards.

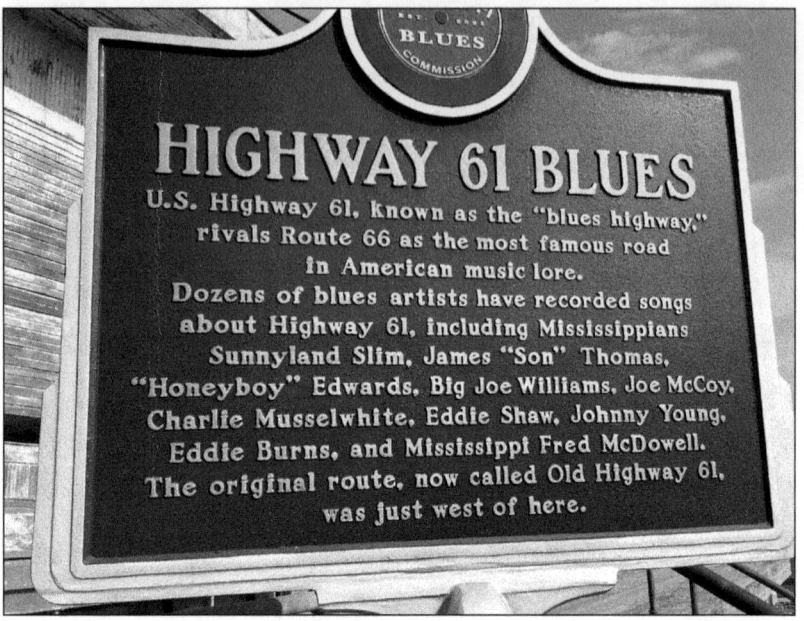

Music was a huge part of the history along the southern Mississippi River. U.S. 61 was called the "blues highway."

Freeze's bike parked with the Confederate cannons at Vicksburg National Military Park.

Bridges across the muddy Mississippi at Natchez, Mississippi.

Entering Louisiana on one of the few good roads. Poor roads ahead!

David Bourg after driving Freeze to New Orleans following the three flats.

Headed home on Amtrak!

RIVER RIDE

Jon Stravers helped Freeze with directions for several days beginning in McGregor, Iowa.

101 degrees on the street thermometer in Alma, Minnesota.

Wall of skis in Pepin, Minnesota, home of Laura Ingalls Wilder.

The Mississippi River in Red Wing, Minnesota.

RIVER RIDE

U.S. 61 closed ahead in St. Paul, Minnesota.

Kim Hyatt and Ethan Horne in St. Paul, Minnesota.

Freeze and Horne didn't let the train blocking the roads north stop them.

The Great River Road signs that Freeze welcomed, especially this one in Little Falls, Minnesota.

The source of the Mississippi River at Lake Itasca State Park, Minnesota.

Freeze and Mike Zachow in Bemidji, Minnesota. Zachow continued to help with directions and logistics for the remainder of the trip.

The Big Fish near Bena, Minnesota, touting a fish restaurant.

Mark and Anita Goellner of Duluth, Minnesota had Freeze over for dinner where he spent the night and got several days of help with his planned route on the way to Minneapolis.

RIVER RIDE

Freeze stopped to visit Postmaster Laurie Dhein twice in her Lutsen, Minnesota post office.

Inside the Grand Portage National Monument.

Bill and Mariann Kuhn. Freeze met them at Grand Portage, the first of many conversations since.

Finally complete, Freeze reached Jackson Square in New Orleans, celebrating the end of the Mississippi River and Lake Superior journey.

DAVID FREEZE

about the author

Having completed most of the main cycling routes across America and all 50 states, David Freeze has a great love of large bodies of water. What better than America's greatest river, the Mightly Mississippi, for his next up-close view of back roads America? Then on to a side visit to the North Shore of Lake Superior! This is Freeze's 10th book. He hasn't been everywhere yet, but it's still on his list!

David is also a motivational speaker, emphasizing that regular people can achieve amazing things. Contact him at david.freeze@ctc.net. Walnut Creek Farm Publishing is named after his farm.

An accomplished runner and endurance cyclist, David has written seven other books that cover various adventures across America by bicycle and another one by historic biplane. David also chronicled a journey across North Carolina while pushing a baby jogger. He has completed almost 97,000 running miles and almost 30,000 endurance cycling miles.

Other books by David Freeze include:

- **Lord, Ride with Me Today**
  The story of a solo coast-to-coast bicycle journey — 2013
- **Pedaling, Prayers and Perseverance**
  35 Days Cycling Solo from Maine to Key West — 2014
- **Riding the Rails to Freedom**
  Cycling the Underground Railroad Route from Alabama to Ontario — 2015
- **Highway to History**
  A Cycling Adventure on Route 66 — 2016
- **Young Again**
  Veterans recapture a moment of youth through
  Ageless Aviation Dreams Foundation — 2017
- **Cycling the Northwest**
  A solo trip from the West Coast to Green Bay, through
  Bigfoot country — 2017
- **One Day at a Time Across North Carolina**
  A Solo Run/Walk Behind a Baby Jogger — 2018
- **Fearless & Determined**
  An epic solo cycling journey from Nevada to Alaska — 2019
- **Crossing America on Convenience Store at a Time**
  A solo cycling journey across the southern U.S. — 2021

www.ingramcontent.com/pod-product-compliance
Lightning Source LLC
Chambersburg PA
CBHW060822050426
42453CB00008B/546